Discover Your Business Destiny:
Co-Creating, Stewarding and Standing to Manifest God's Divine Plan

ISBN: 979-8-218-96206-7

PUBLISHED BY:
Bralynn Newby International, LLC
Southern Pines, NC 28387
Support@BralynnNewby.com

Cover art by David Muñoz, DavidMunozArt.com
and Midjourney art by Elizabeth Gomes, EcclesiaofBurningOnes.com

DISCOVER *Your* BUSINESS *Destiny*

Co-Creating, Stewarding and Standing to Manifest God's Divine Plan

BRALYNN NEWBY

ENDORSEMENTS

Bralynn has taken one of heaven's best kept secrets and revealed it for all to see and use! This book is inspiring, informative and inclusive. A must read for any and all business owners that want to see their business explode in ways that the human mind alone cannot perceive. She has taken concepts that could be seen as complicated and made them accessible and attainable. It is easy to understand and implement. No matter what stage you find yourself in the marketplace, this information is sure to propel you to the next level!

—Dr. Candace Benton, Ph.D., LCSW
Business Owner

I have been blessed and honored to have known Bralynn as a personal friend for several years. She is a forerunner of forerunners. She is blazing trails that are unknown to most both in the natural and spirit realms. This book is not only based on her years of research, but mostly from her personal experience through her deep levels of intimacy with the Holy Trinity, and life-changing levels of wisdom and revelation, which have been entrusted to her from the Throne. Do not think that this is just a book about building a successful business, but a blueprint that holds keys for success in every area of your life. The scripture that comes to mind is 3 John 1-2, "Beloved, I pray that you may prosper in all things and be in health, just as your soul prospers."

—Terry Spencer, Chief Heavenly Legislator
RevolutionGlory.com

Becoming spirit-centered and tapping into your creative design of spirit, soul and body allows you to exercise and strengthen every aspect of who you really are. Bralynn unfolds the design of our Creator with leading edge insight and wisdom to develop your business potential. In this book you will discover and learn ways to master who you are, become what you were created to be and do, and develop business success with spiritual gifts, talents and creative insight that will help supercharge a normal business into achieving growth and success never before thought possible. Come along with Bralynn and step into a whole new world of business development, taking the limits off of your potential to become a Spirit-Centered business!

—Timothy Bence, Minister to the King,
Global Development Entrepreneur

DEDICATION

In memory of Christopher Paul Carter, whose childlike wonder and adventurous heart brought me into the heavenly realms to meet Jesus face to face. I wouldn't be as far as I am on my journey with the Lord, or be doing what I do without your fun loving friendship and teaching.

Sail on, Navigator!

DEDICATION

ACKNOWLEDGEMENTS

Diann Newby: Mom who believes in me even though she doesn't get what I do

Reagan Loughry: Brilliant get-'er-done girl, connecter extraordinaire, and fellow adventurer

Miranda Wendler: Powerful prayer warrior and inspiring friend

Donna Neeper: Steady ship of wise counsel and partner in awakening the body of Christ

Daniel Duval: Spiritual strategy forerunner and mentor ...and now pastor

John Graham: Spiritual father "Papa John", my biggest cheerleader

Rex Andagan: Faithful podcast producer and techy right hand

Thank you all so much. You make my life rich.

This book in your hands has been prayed over and infused with blessings and the frequency of heaven.

Enjoy!

FOREWORD

by Virginia Killingsworth

Since you have opened the pages of this book, you are, no doubt, a signpost of the massive shift that is taking place in the earth, in the cosmos and in the consciousness of all mankind. Perhaps you have experienced the necessary dissatisfaction that comes between the death of the old and the emergence of the new. Maybe you have received glimpses of this new thing deep within your heart yet are wondering how to usher it from the invisible realm and into tangibility. Let me assure you that you are in a good place, no matter how uncomfortable it may feel. Let me also assure you that the keys contained in this book will help to answer your questions... even those questions which are not fully formed within you.

It was a similar quest that prompted me to write *Miracles Are Normal: Co-Creating Through Oneness With God.* On this journey of learning to manifest miracles, I have seen many "impossibilities" fade away. I have witnessed the lavish goodness of the Father materialize through the renewed thoughts, healed emotions, sanctified imagination, and bold declarations of those who dared to co-create with the Creator. I've been leading groups to explore the limitlessness of the heavenly realm for over a decade and am encouraged to see God's sons waking up and rising up to enjoy ALL that was purchased for us on the cross of Christ.

The practical aspects of owning a business and creating wealth from heaven to earth are topics that have been largely neglected in past seasons, but these truths are now being strategically released here in this book "for such a time as this." Bralynn is a forerunner, not only in co-creating with God, but also in stewarding business and wealth for His Kingdom.

I met Bralynn through a mutual friend who was one of her coaching clients. In a very short time, I noticed tremendous positive transformation in my friend's life and business as a result of their work together. Bralynn has ministered at our local ecclesia, *All Things Restored*, and has imparted strategic wisdom that has helped us to see more clearly and function more effectively. She has an uncanny ability to soar high in the Spirit while simultaneously solidifying the realm of encounter, making the spiritual practical. Bralynn can make even the deepest spiritual concepts so simple that a child can enter in. Her skill, knowledge and expertise flow through a heart of love for others, revealing obscured destinies, removing blockages to success, and giving those around her wings to fly.

On a personal level, Bralynn has become a dear and trusted friend. She has poured tirelessly and selflessly into my life and ministry, always challenging me to become my best self, always encouraging me to soar a little higher, always cheering me on in my destiny.

As you read this book, Bralynn's warm, conversational style will make you feel like you're sitting with her at the kitchen table. Her humor will make devouring this work a delight. With practical examples, she will take you by the hand and lead you into new and exciting spiritual territory. But most of all, profound, practical and life-changing truths are presented in a clear and concise manner, allowing you to start at the very beginning and to step right into the destiny and abundance the Father has planned for you.

Often, we grasp the concept of spiritual truths but have trouble understanding what those truths are to look like in daily life. In this book, Bralynn breaks down that barrier completely, as she vividly describes her own personal journey in the heavenly realm, gently guiding you with questions that will engage your spirit and ignite your imagination. She will walk you through receiving, reading and engaging your destiny scroll. She will help you to understand your mandate, mission and vision. She will help you to properly establish your business in heaven with your Declaration of Trade and your Deed of Commerce and Trade...and SO much more!

I enjoyed and learned from reading *Discover Your Business Destiny*, and I know you will too. I plan to use the Prayers and Declarations on a regular basis, knowing that as I do the work in the heavenly realm, it will manifest in the earth...bringing about an expansion and multiplication of all that the Father has entrusted to me. Everyone has been given something to steward for God's glory, so everyone would benefit tremendously from reading this book. And if you will utilize the truths and tools presented here, there is no limit to what God will do through you!

Never doubt God's mighty power to work in you and accomplish all this. He will achieve infinitely more than your greatest request, your most unbelievable dream, and exceed your wildest imagination! He will outdo them all, for his miraculous power constantly energizes you.

—Ephesians 3:20 (TPT)

To the Miraculous You!
Virginia Killingsworth

Founder and Senior Leader of *All Things Restored* ecclesia, Jacksonville, FL
AllThingsRestored.org

Founder and Senior Leader of *Tekhelet Restored* global community
TekheletRestored.org

Author, Speaker, Worship Leader, Creator of *Miracles Are Normal Online Course*
VirginiaKillingsworth.com

TABLE OF CONTENTS

SECTION 2
PRAYERS AND DECLARATIONS
TO STEWARD AND STAND

SECTION THREE
CONCLUSION AND WHAT'S NEXT

PREFACE

Purpose and Backstory

The world is shifting, changing, accelerating. Technology is doubling in capability every 12-18 months. The way we do life and interact with others doesn't even resemble what it did three years ago. The root of these global shifts is spiritual. Nothing can manifest in our physical experience without it first becoming real in someone's mind...which is actually the "spirit realm" or "quantum field". In fact, with the discoveries of quantum physics, we now understand that the entire structure of the physical realm is actually much different than what we can currently grasp or understand using the Newtonian physics we're used to operating in.

Yet, we are trying to do business the same way we were taught, and pretty much the same way it's been done for the last 50 years, to be conservative. As we gain revelation and understanding of ourselves as spiritual beings having this earthly experience, we are awakening to spiritual principles and how to properly engage them. This book is a taste of what we are discovering, exploring and implementing in Spirit-Centered Business™. My desire is that it will open your eyes to the possibilities of doing business differently, and ultimately, to doing life differently. Doing it from the heavenly realms. Doing it Spirit-Centered™.

When you are spirit-centered, you are in alignment. Your head and heart—your intellect and passion, are in alignment, and you are aligned with God's purposes and plans for your life and your business. You are operating in your true identity—who your Creator says you are. You are also aligned with spiritual principles, and in alignment and harmony with others. Your being is properly positioned with your spirit dominant, then your soul, and lastly your body. Internal, vertical, and horizontal alignment is your power position. Being truly spirit-centered also means that you are aware of the spirit realm, and can access its resources, wisdom, counsel, strategies, and help to fulfill your mission here on earth. Even though our ancestors knew more about how to interact with other realms and dimensions, these ancient mysteries are now being revealed to us for present day life. We are just beginning to understand the wealth of assistance and guidance available to us in the heavenly realm. A foundational tenet of Spirit-Centered Business™ is to be in **Alignment**, effectively use your authorized **Access**, and implement tools and strategies for maximum **Impact** across the globe for the Kingdom of God. That way you can fully walk out your destiny and leave the legacy you were designed to create.

At the same time we're awakening to the power we have to influence the world around us, we're also discovering there are forces being used against us to keep us from doing just that. Well, maybe it's more that we're waking up to the depth of evil and how it is woven into the fabric of our culture and even into our DNA and psyche. We're also getting new revelations on the tools and technology the enemy uses against us and, more importantly, how to nullify them in the spirit realm and protect ourselves. Walking out our destiny requires knowing and operating in our true identity, as well as understanding the schemes of our foe. Forces of darkness—our adversary and his ilk, have hidden, obfuscated, stolen and tricked us and our ancestors into trading away both our destinies and our identities. This book shares hard won intel I've gathered, technologies I've discovered, and how to uncover, unlock, and take back the truth of who you are and what you're on this earth to do.

Do I do it perfectly? Pffffft no. But I am practicing, pressing forward and not settling or shrinking back. When you confidently walk in your true powerful identity, you will be more focused on going after the magnitude and beauty of your dreams. You will play a bigger game in life, and I am your biggest cheerleader! You, dear reader, are part of my destiny. The more I help you fulfill yours, the more I fulfill mine. Let's do this!

How to Use this Book

While you may only need to read through the training once, the prayers and declarations are meant to be a repeated exercise. As you engage your destiny scroll by nurturing it with these prayers and position yourself in the infinite potential and possibility of the spirit realm, your 3D world will begin to change and align with the spiritual world you're creating. **Saying these prayers just one time won't help in**

the long run. It happens with repetition over time. We explore how the spiritual principle of transformation works in the Declarations section. Prepare for an exciting journey!

Being a bit of a "jumper" myself, you may notice that I repeat important concepts for those who jump to a section of interest rather than reading front to back. Don't roll your eyes at me...it's all good. LOL!

CHAPTER 1

INTRODUCTION

For the purposes of this book, and as a philosophy to which I subscribe, I define "Destiny" as God's perfect plan for your life for which He designed you to have the capacity, privilege and responsibility to co-create with Him. Our destiny is bigger than us, bigger than our mortal lives, and extends beyond the limits of our 3D existence. There's a beautiful and sometimes complicated dance between holding a magical sense of wonderment and expectation for the adventure, and doggedly holding on to your dreams with persistent tenacity and focus. Your ability to hold the raindrops and light beams of life in balance determines how well you dance. I hope to inspire you to believe in your dreams and be amazed and overjoyed when they don't come true...when you actually get something better.

"Life is a journey, not a destination."

—Ralph Waldo Emerson

Even though I label section one "Training", it's really meant to give you an opportunity to explore the possibilities. This is not a formula, and there are certainly no claims nor guarantees of success. Prince Charming is not going to rescue you, although he might. You're not going to win the lottery, or maybe you will. I'll share stories of results from doing this work, and extol the virtues of sticking with it. But ultimately, the choice and the experience are up to you, dear reader. I suspect there are more paths to take you to receiving your destiny scroll, "reading" it, making a plan to get you there, and then taking the daily action steps to walk it out. This is just the one God led me to discover, and I've implemented with Him. I heard a guy say, "When something works it's easy to be fooled into believing that's THE way to do it. It's just one way, a way that happened to work." That stuck with me. Take with you that which fits, and leave behind anything that doesn't.

Reassurances for Both the "Spiritual" and the "Religious"

I come from a Judeo-Christian background, and have an intimate relationship with God in all 3 of His personhoods, Father/Yahweh, Son/Yeshua (Jesus), and Holy Spirit/ Ruach. My goal is not to preach to you or convert you, and especially not to thump you over the head with a bible. I've had enough of that, and, frankly, it's a huge turn-off. I'm done with churchianity, and the feel-good, socially accept-able drivel that comes out of some pulpits. That is not to say there aren't exceptional churches doing amazing things. That is also not saying I don't respect traditional church. What I learned there laid a lot of the foundation I've built on in my own faith journey. For me, I have made far more progress in my spiritual journey outside the four walls of church. I just ask that you have an open, non-judgemental mind as you read this, because then God can help you. Also, don't throw the baby out with the bathwater. If there's something you don't agree with or understand, ignore it and just use what works for you.

I'm not a bible scholar, although I have studied, and continue to study God's written word almost daily. I also believe God didn't stop speaking, and His wisdom can be found in everything He created. (He spoke through a donkey; He can speak through a "non-believer"!) While some of the ideas in this book are extra-biblical, nothing I share will be anti-biblical. I encourage you to go to Father and ask for yourself if you come across anything new or contrary to what you currently believe. Unfortunately a lot of misguided agenda has crept into various translations of the bible, so I also recommend going all the way back to the Hebrew or Greek, (or even Paleo Hebrew or Aramaic) and frame it in the original context and culture of the day. For instance, when Peter was miraculously freed from prison and went to his friend's home, their FIRST response was that it wasn't Peter, but his angel. What does that tell you? They were used to seeing angels, and knew they looked like their humans! This isn't explicitly spelled out, but can easily be inferred. Now, I'll be the first to admit that I do NOT know how all of this works. Like everyone else who is venturing into spiritual territory, I'm mapping it out as I go, and there are pieces of the puzzle yet to be revealed and understood. So I ask for grace, as I try to give you as much as I currently have. I'm sure at some point this book will be obsolete, but this is my mandate right now, and you are not reading this by accident.

That being said, I will try my best to note where a reference may be found in the bible for things I say. On the other hand, because I honor those of you who are spiritual, but may not know Yeshua, I will use language and references to spiritual principles and practices that may sound "New Age". Usually, I use words that express an experience I've had because there isn't a better word to describe it—not because I want to trigger anybody! I also don't want to shy away from perfectly good, honest words that have been tainted in some way. For instance, in the song "Deck the Halls", we all know that "Don we now our gay apparel" does NOT mean we dress like transvestites! Please. Let's just have an adult conversation, and not get our knickers in a swivel. So, regarding the prayers and declarations in this book, feel free to use whatever salutation you choose to address our Higher Power. I'll agree to switch up how I refer to God, and you can agree to just change it if you prefer something else. Deal?

That said, in the interest of bridging people still in the Church age over to the Kingdom age, I admit that I may weigh a bit heavy on tying ideas back to their biblical foundations. If you don't like that, tough. It's my book. (Big cherubic smile!)

Transparency About My Conundrum

Okay, now, here's my transparent moment. I am in a conundrum as to how to approach this subject matter. I know God is calling me to reveal amazing, transformative truths, and I also know that both sides of the aisle have been hurt by the other. I have precious spiritual friends who have been wounded by the church and condemned by

Christians. And I have dear friends and family, myself included, who have felt slimed and creeped out by overly zealous New Agers and others. My heart is for unity, and to share what I've learned to help you in your business. The problem I'm having is that I know the authority and power of my position as seated on my throne in heaven was given to me by Yeshua. I can't deny that fact. Nor can I advocate using the principles I'm going to share with you outside of His permission.

John 10:1 says "Most assuredly, I say to you, he who does not enter the sheepfold by the door, but climbs up some other way, the same is a thief and a robber."

You see, within His Kingdom, we operate by grace and freedom. Anyone outside God's Kingdom may still operate in spiritual principles, but it's by law. There's a price to be paid for power, and you won't have legal authority. You'll be that thief and robber. When you accept Jesus as your Lord who paid that price for you, you can come boldly to the throne. If you usurp God's protocol, you have to pay your own price. That's just the way it works, so what can I do? Additionally, the majority of the promises God makes are specifically for His people...those who accept Yeshua as Lord and honor His payment for us. (There is a prayer in the Bonus Prayer section toward the end if you would like to do this at any time.)

My heart is breaking as I write this because I feel so torn. I'm called to set captives free, which means awakening believers to their power AND helping spiritual people understand how to do business supernaturally. I don't think it's an either-or thing, it's a both-and. Yet, I don't want anyone to get hurt, or oppressed, or tormented, or have to pay a price Yeshua already paid. He said it was done. Done means done. Really. So, please, dear reader—know that you are totally and completely loved REGARDLESS of which side of the fence you're on. God loves you SO much, and wants you to fulfill your personal destiny, and to fulfill the destiny of your business that He is allowing me to write this from my heart. Please receive the love, joy, and peace frequencies infused with the heartfelt intent to bless your socks off as you read and implement this book. Know that every page, and every word has been prayed over and infused with life.

In fact, let me pray over you right now, as you embark on the journey of learning and implementing this book.

My Prayer for You

Father, I come to you in the mighty name of Yeshua. I honor you and praise you for giving me this assignment, and I declare your glory is released through every word on every page. I thank you that you know in advance everyone whose lives and businesses this book will touch, and I dedicate it to you and to them. I pray they would come into a deeper understanding of who you created them to be, and what you created their business to be. I ask for a new level of spiritual awakening to come upon these brilliant business people. Lord, let there be angels and heavenly protectors to guard their hearts and minds as they train and activate this teaching. I declare that there will be no hindrances to their capacity or willingness to receive your truth. If there are any areas where they have been held back or locked away from seeing or receiving their destiny scroll or walking it out, I call for freedom right now. Let them embrace more of the fullness of their identity as spiritual beings, and let them grasp the importance and significance of their walking out the destiny of their business. Give them clarity on what it looks like to administrate their divine assignment and what they are truly called to do. Please stir up your Spirit in them and speak directly to their hearts. Let them feel and know your amazing love for them. Give them peace and a comforting rest and assuredness that you are a good God—the God above all other gods, and are seated on your throne. I pray this standing in the power given to me by your son, Yeshua Hamashiach. (Jesus, the Messiah's proper Hebrew name.)

SECTION ONE
Training and Equipping for Your Destiny

CHAPTER 2

ACCESS

I don't pray the way I used to. In 2017 I went to a conference with Robert Henderson and Dr. Faisal Malick that began a shift in my awareness of our ability and invitation to step into the spirit realm of Father's Kingdom. I learned that we can and are called to enter the courtrooms of Heaven to bring cases before the righteous Judge, God. Shortly thereafter Christopher Paul Carter taught me to turn my focus into the Kingdom realm around us to build relationships with Jesus, Father and Holy Spirit. Talking with them while sitting on a swing or strolling through heavenly gardens, I realized "prayer" would never be the same.

"You can pass through his open gates with the password of praise. Come right into his presence with thanksgiving. Come bring your thank offering to him and affectionately bless his beautiful name! For Yahweh is always good and ready to receive you. He's so loving that it will amaze you—so kind that it will astound you!"

—Psalm 100: 4-5a (TPT)

"So above all, constantly seek God's Kingdom and his righteousness, then all these less important things will be given to you abundantly."

—Matt 6:33 (TPT)

The way I've come to receive and access my destiny scrolls or books, and help my clients do the same is by "closing my physical eyes and opening the eyes of my heart", as Christopher Carter says. This is the "stepping in" access we will use throughout this book and in your daily routine to manifest your destiny, should you choose to go for it. (And, of course, I recommend you go after it with everything you've got!)

So let's talk about the WHY, the HOW and the Protocols of access.

WHY: Five Reasons to Access the Spirit Realm

(Heaven, God's Kingdom, specifically.)

1. Intimacy

It's about nurturing your relationship with your Creator and Source, God. Or Father, Jesus and Holy Spirit, if you engage with all three persons of the Godhead.

All of heaven is relational, so nothing happens outside of relationship. You will better understand yourself when you get to know who Jesus is. Walking in the fullness of who you are requires oneness with God. I'm not including a lot of teaching on this here, I'm just stating that seeking intimacy with Yahweh and His Kingdom must be first in your life if you are to fully know who you are and walk out your destiny. Everything else in your life and business will flow out of this relationship.

As in Matthew 6:33: *"But first and most importantly seek (aim at, strive after) His Kingdom and His righteousness [His way of doing and being right—the attitude and character of God], and all these things will be given to you also."* (AMP)

If you prefer to think of God as Source or Love, or Creator, or even just Higher Power, no worries! All of those are true and He will meet you where you are. He loves you that much.

The point here is to intentionally connect and spend time in that presence. Let that love envelope you and nurture you on a regular basis.

2. Identity

You are more powerful than you can even imagine!

When you can spend time with your Creator you can better understand how He created you. You can also get a better handle on where you came from. We are spirit beings, and were given a soul and put into a physical body to be able to interact with this 3-dimensional world we are sojourning through.

When we let go of the limitations that keep us stuck and step into the Truth of who and what we are (pure energy, light and power—in the image of our Creator), we can soar! We have the capacity and permission to co-create the future we envision for ourselves on our destiny scroll. Understanding and operating in your true, unfiltered identity is so critical to fulfilling your destiny that you will see it come up in several areas of this book.

"Whenever you ask God about purpose,
He's always going to answer you about identity.
He doesn't want your assignment to usurp your identity,
so He needs to make sure you know who you are before you
set out on your mission."

—Dr. Faisal Malick

3. Citizenship

Know what heaven is like.

Hebrews 12:23 says we are citizens of Heaven. How can we say we're citizens if we don't even know what it's like? We've been praying, "Your Kingdom come, your will be done on earth as it is in heaven," in the Lord's Prayer for 2,000 years. So how would we know what "as it is in heaven" looks like unless we actually look at it? John 5:19 says that Jesus only did what he saw his heavenly Father doing. If we're supposed to do as Jesus did, we need to see what Father is doing as well. Implementing what you learn in this book will help you manifest on earth what you see/hear/perceive/experience in heaven.

4. Legal Paperwork/Authority

We need legal paperwork such as our mantle, mandate, scroll, and other establishing documents from heaven if we're to fully live out our destiny.

This may be new to some of you, so let me flesh it out a bit, and tie these concepts to "normal" business ideas.

Mantles

A mantle is a covering that represents God-given authority for a specific assignment. It's very important that you ask for and receive a mantle to step out and do what you want to do in your business. Don't get too caught up in this though, because oftentimes our mantle comes along with our mandate or calling, and we don't necessarily receive it separately.

The problem only comes with either operating without a mantle of authority, or operating with a false mantle. False mantles can be unwittingly received if someone puts it on you. Usually these are well-meaning people who pray for you or give you a prophetic word that Father never intended for you. It can also happen when parents want their children to take over the family business without checking to see if that's what the Creator wants. If something doesn't feel right, don't accept it in the spirit realm. Always ask God if this word is for you, and if it's for you right now.

If you feel you've been carrying a false mantle, simply pray:

Father, forgive me for taking on an assignment that's not mine. I give it back to you, and break agreement with it. I receive my forgiveness and declare myself free and clear of any hold that false mantle had over my life. I request in its place, the authentic mantle of authority for the destiny you designed for me. I receive this true mantle and the responsibility attached to it in the powerful name of Jesus. Amen.

Mandates

Mandates are your overarching calling or purpose. They are inherently connected to our wiring and destiny. Usually your mandate is fulfilled through various assignments and missions throughout your life. While we all have common mandates as believers in Christ, such as "preach the good news" or "heal the sick, cast out demons and raise the dead," you have your own unique mandate specific to your design and destiny. It's very important that you do the work to find out what that is if you don't already know.

It may come to you slowly, in bits and pieces as you increase your understanding of your identity and destiny. Mine did. I needed to be able to clearly articulate my identity before I could understand my mandate, which is, "I release voices held captive by fear and doubt."

This is innately connected to my story, my wiring and my destiny because it wasn't safe for me to voice my opinion if it differed from the "party line". I spent too much time in fear, and my heart breaks for people who have also had their voices shut down. I became a protector of the weak and a fighter for justice.

Then, years later, I was reading Luke 11:23 and had a vision of my hand sweeping over the globe and gathering people's influence for the purpose of returning it to them. That's when I realized there was more to my mandate. I added the second part, "...and recover and restore lost, stolen, traded away, abandoned or deteriorated influence." In that moment I knew I had a role to play in people's destiny. Specifically in awakening and activating *influencers* into their identity and calling. This also speaks to my warrior spirit and my desire for significance in my life. (I was an actress on and off for 30 years. Big courtesy with a flourish.) ☺

Ask for your mandate to be revealed to you. The Destiny Mapping exercises later in this book may help you unearth this treasure.

How do Mandates Correspond to our Mission and Vision?

First, a clarification on what Mission and Vision are, as some may not be familiar with the difference.

"This is war, and whoever is not on my side is against me, and whoever does not gather the spoils with me will be forever scattered."

—Luke 11:23 TPT

What spoils of war are you called to gather?

Mission: Who you serve and what you do to serve them to get to your vision.

Vision: This is the ideal future state of your business. (More on this in the Destiny Scroll section.)

Let's look at an example of how these three work together.

Mandate: I am a restorer of streets with dwellings.

Corresponding Mission Statement:

As a property manager I work with owners and tenants to revitalize low income neighborhoods.

Subsequent Vision Statement:

We are the premiere property management company sought out by owners who are inspired by our excellent track record of neighborhood revitalization, and want the same for their properties and neighborhoods. Properties we manage are highly rated and sought after by tenants who want to be a part of a safe, thriving community.

Establishing Documents

After you've received the destiny scroll for your business (coming soon, I promise!) you will need to establish your business in the spirit realm by filing a *Declaration of Trade** with the heavenly Court of Titles and Deeds. This document presents evidence that you have the right to operate this business according to Kingdom principles. It assumes you've already received your Mantle—your God-given authority to be a business owner, and your Mandate—your God-given assignment. The Declaration of Trade is your legal agreement to partner with Heaven. It also includes the Deed of Commerce and Trade, which establishes your trading floor, or place of business on earth and in the heavenly realms. It gives you the right to the following:

- Heavenly resources and tools
- Angelic assistance and assistants
- Direction on strategy and tactics
- Divine connections
- Protection
- The opportunity to operate in spiritual principles (even the supernatural ones!)
- ...and more to be revealed!

There are other establishing documents you might need particular to your business or industry. Working with clients we've come across documents such as building permits, signage permits, demolition permits, or licenses to divert traffic or publicly gather. Heaven will tell you what you need. Whatever document you need on earth should also be first created in heaven. That way, when it's created on earth it will already have a stamp of approval and carry the frequency of heaven for divine favor.

You may wish to create your Declaration of Trade by going through our online course. Click the Resources tab on SpiritCenteredBusiness.com.

5. Resources and Protection

The 5th reason you would want access to God's Kingdom realm is for resources and protection. Even if you don't have a business these are always needed to fulfill your personal destiny. They are doubly important when you are building a market-share-taking, culture-shifting entity that transforms people's lives!

If you're like me, you weren't taught to actually approach Yahweh's throne when you needed something. (see Heb 4:16) You were probably taught to pray from wherever you were, and hope He heard you. I also missed the lessons in church on how to co-create from heaven. In case you did too, the great news is that we can! We are made in His image, as in Gen 1:27, and he's a creator. 1 John 4:17 says "As He is, so are we in this world." We are also seated with Christ in Heavenly places. (see Eph 2:6)

We were taught to pray from separation, but if you've accepted Jesus into your heart, you are no longer separated. Actually you're never separated, it's just an illusion...but the fact that you become a new creation (see Cor 5:17) means you now have that union of oneness with Father, your Source and Creator because Ruach Hakodesh (Holy Spirit) lives inside you.

Point being, when you're operating in your true identity, you can receive resources and protection at a whole new level by accessing heaven.

HOW to Enter into the Spiritual Realm

Imagination, the Eyes of Your Heart

> "Logic will get you from A to B. Imagination will take you everywhere."
>
> —Albert Einstein

In order to receive your destiny scroll and then read it, you'll need to access heaven, where it is kept. Our imagination is the tool our Creator gave us to connect with Him and the rest of His Kingdom. Paul says, "I pray that the *eyes of your heart* may be enlightened in order that you may know the hope to which He has called you, the riches of His glorious inheritance in His holy people." —Eph 1:18 (NIV, emphasis mine) These are your spiritual eyes, and you can include ears here too.

"Seeing" includes all your spiritual senses: hearing, smelling, tasting, touching as well as perceiving, or just knowing something when you check in or ask a question.

Here are some scriptures to ground this out:

- John 10 speaks a lot about *hearing* and *knowing* our Shepherd's voice.
- John 5:19 says Jesus did what He *saw* Father doing.
- Psalm 34:8 says, "*Taste* and see that the Lord is good."
- Matthew 10:7 (TPT) "And as you go, preach this message: 'Heaven's Kingdom realm is accessible, close enough *to touch*.'"
- When Jesus asked Peter who he thought He was, Peter answered, "You are the Christ, the Son of the living God." and Jesus replied, "Blessed are you, Simon son of Jonah! For this was not revealed to you by flesh and blood, but by My Father in heaven. " (Mat 16:16-17) He just had a *knowing*.

You may have been told that imagination is just for children's fantasies. Well, Mark 10:15 says, "Truly I tell you, anyone who will not receive the Kingdom of God like a little child will never enter it." We have to have our wonder and awe and creativity revived, and set our over-analyzing minds on the shelf.

Remember that we are spirit beings, we have a soul—the seat of our primary mind, will and emotions, and we live in a body. We are designed to operate in heavenly places as well as on earth. Typically we've not been taught about living from or as our spirit. We've been conditioned to live primarily out of our soul. But our soul isn't designed to access the spirit realm, so I recommend transitioning into your spirit when you do this work.

It really helps to call your spirit forward into the driver's seat, have your soul take a rest in the backseat, and ask Father to sanctify your imagination. Ask to see only His Kingdom, and set a hedge around your imagination so that nothing that is not of God may enter. In fact, because of the work I do now with my clients and in my ekklesia groups, (administrating and legislating God's assignments), Yahweh has instructed me to always put up a barrier with camouflage so I am operating completely in stealth mode, undetectable by the enemy.

For me, and I think for most people, the soul to spirit switch is like a rheostat, rather than a toggle. There are degrees of connectedness on the way from soul to spirit. The imagination is a great gate opener to start the rheostat moving toward fully operating from your spirit. You can start visualizing the scene, get oriented, and then see where it takes you. You'll know you're operating more by your spirit when your personal preferences and opinions about whatever is going on diminish. But until you get there, it's perfectly fine to choose things to suit you as you're exploring and co-creating in the spirit realm.

Here's a funny story. I was leading a small group in a "Kinging Up" activation to see themselves as kings. When we got to the part where we looked down to see our shoes one of the girls exclaimed, "Oh, no!" Afterward she explained that she was shocked to look down and see bright yellow "Aladdin" slippers with huge curled up toes. She wanted to get them off right away, and asked for something more her style. She looked again and saw black Doc Martin boots, and was very happy. It would have been interesting to ask why she saw the slippers...note to self if you see something unexpected, be sure to ask about it!

You'll find more about visualizing or intentionally directing your imagination a bit later. We'll go into more advanced quantum work in the next chapter.

Protocol: Spirit Realm Basics

When I first started stepping into the heavenly realm—which is really just turning your focus to the spirit realm around you and actually *in* you, I needed reassurance that I was safe. As soon as I saw the scene I asked Jesus where He was in it, so I could focus on him. I still like to make sure he's around...he is the door, afterall. (see John 10:9) I suggest inviting Father, Jesus, and/or Holy Spirit to be your tour guide. As you practice shifting your awareness and "visiting" heaven, God may introduce you to other angels or members of the cloud of witnesses. It's fine to engage with them, but I advise keeping your eyes on Jesus.

"And now we are brothers and sisters in God's family
because of the blood of Jesus, and he welcomes us to come
into the most holy sanctuary in the heavenly realm—boldly
and without hesitation. For he has dedicated a new, life-
giving way for us to approach God. For just as the veil was
torn in two, Jesus' body was torn open to give us free and
fresh access to him!"

—Heb 10:19-20 (TPT)

If you have unwittingly seen into the spirit realm and witnessed darkness, as often happens to children, you may also want to be very specific about stepping ONLY into Father's Kingdom. I've worked with people who had negative experiences as children and shut down their capacity to see by making an inner vow not to. If there is freemasonry in your family line, your ancestors may have taken a vow not to see as well. You may need to break that off before you can fully interact. I'd be happy to help. Just visit SpiritCenteredBusiness.com/healing and book a session.

In case you jumped here without reading the intro, I talked more about why you want to honor heaven's protocol. You may wish to go back and read that. Stay safe.

CHAPTER 3

ALIGNMENT

Align with your True Identity

We are spiritual beings on earth for a purpose, and we are powerful far beyond our understanding.

"We are here to awaken to the reality of our true identity—that we are sparks of the Eternal Imperishable Spirit, who is the Source of all Creation and the very essence of our being."

—Shriram Sharma

We are God's BEST idea! He created us in His image to carry His characteristics wherever we go here on earth. Each of us expresses a unique facet of His essence. We are magnificently designed, treasured and beloved. When you accept the gift of Jesus' redemption through His death, burial and resurrection, you can step into sonship and kingship. "Son" is not a gender—it's a positional title. The whole universe is breathlessly waiting for us to mature and take our rightful place as Sons upon the earth. Romans 8:19 says *"For the anxious longing of the creation waits eagerly for the revealing of the sons of God."* (NASB)

Sons inherit. Sons have access without a guest pass. Sons can raid the fridge!

The topic of identity is very near and dear to me, and I have taught and coached A LOT on it. The number one goal of the enemy is to keep us from knowing and operating in our true identity. For the purposes of this book, I only want to stress that the more alignment your thoughts and actions have with who you truly are, the more you will be able to fulfill your destiny, and that of your business.

So let's get into a little bit of how we can totally be deceived about who we are, or dumbed down to thinking we're unworthy, powerless and hopeless.

One main way is trauma that happens in childhood. We make assumptions and tie things together that weren't meant to go together, and make inner vows to protect ourselves. Even later in life trauma and soul woundings can cause us to assign false meaning to events or other people's actions. The narratives we create allow false identity thoughts to turn into patterns of behavior or coping mechanisms based on lies. These become the structure of our inner world.

One of the deep lies I've worked on, and potentially still have layers to peel off, is fear of someone getting upset. I equated someone's angry outbursts with lies like, "It's my fault. I can't do anything right. I'm not good enough. They don't love me. I'm unloveable. I have to make them happy. I'm not safe." And more...you get the picture. (Cancel the agreement and clear the energy of reading these negatives.) Do you see how these lies would make me a people pleaser, a conflict avoider, a hider, a peacekeeper, non-boat-rocker at all costs? With those filters on, I didn't take risks, I didn't express my opinion, and I didn't have a voice. So how could I fulfill my destiny?

Shedding false beliefs about yourself is a critical step in truly walking out who you were created to be and making the impact you were designed to make in the world. It's the first step in my business coaching process, and one we come back to every time we come across something not working right. Start with identity. What are you believing— even subconsciously—that's holding you back, self sabotaging, or keeping you in a cycle.

The great news is, there are many ways to do this, and you don't have to do it alone. In fact, in most cases, you can't do it alone. You're the picture in the frame, so how can you see the frame? There's no shame in it, just grab a coach or therapist and get 'er done. We all have schtuff to let go of.

Align Your Destinies

Our business destiny, and any other undertaking's destiny, must be in alignment with personal destiny.

To me, it's a tragedy to work at building a business that doesn't truly fulfill you. To settle—and then stay settled. To toil and strive for something for money or because it was the thing in front of you, or because someone said you should do it. To me...that smacks of "fate". (Not to split hairs.)

As I write this I literally just got off a discovery call with someone who thinks they're supposed to start a business in an industry they know nothing about, they've never been interested in before, haven't even taken the time to see what it entails, and certainly have no passion for. Tragic. To my mind, they weren't hearing from God, they just got caught up in someone else's dream and said, "I'll do that too."

Not wanting to totally shut them down, I encouraged them to pretend they were a client looking for that service and see who they found to provide it. Then see where there are gaps in the service, or how they could serve the client better. At least doing this research would show them what the industry is all about. Maybe they would get confirmation one way or the other... But above all...I highly recommended getting the destiny scroll for the business our Creator is calling them to start.

See, the business we're called to must be in alignment with our own personal destiny. We're designed to desire the things on our scroll...they speak to us—call to us even. Our personal destiny will include talents, giftings and experiences that play into the destiny of our business at least in part, if not directly. I'm not saying a career in one thing means you can't pivot to a totally different industry. I'm saying there are common threads woven throughout—if you're on your authentic destiny. All bets are off if you went to college for a degree your parents chose and you hated it then and then hated the job you got after. Clearly, a shift to your true passion is in order in that case!

If you don't have your business destiny scroll yet, or are still unpacking it, look for clues in what made you come alive in the past. What fuels you, rather than drains you? Look for the alignment. Or as some say...follow your heart.

Align with Spiritual Laws/ Kingdom Principles

"We want spiritual principles to be more than beautiful abstractions; we want them to actually transform our lives."

—Marianne Williamson

Spiritual principles are as absolute and binding as gravity. No matter what, if you drop something, it falls to the ground. It's a law. The law of lift supersedes it to allow an airplane to fly, but it doesn't cancel out gravity. Spiritual principles, or universal laws—another common name— work the same way. They always work, regardless of who uses them, unless superseded.

These are the unspoken laws, the suspected laws that take discipline and consistency to prove out using scientific methods. Usually you reap exactly what you sow, like planting a corn seed and getting a corn plant, but sometimes in the spirit realm the harvest looks a little different. Sometimes planting a kindness reaps an opportunity, for example. (But even that could be boiled down to sowing favor and reaping favor.) That's why only careful tracking could attempt to "prove" them. But, regardless...they are real, and they work.

The following, far from a complete list, are some of the more important spiritual laws and Kingdom principles to know in business, in no particular order of importance.

- Sowing and Reaping
  - "Do not be deceived; God is not mocked, for you reap whatever you sow."
  —Gal 6:7 (emphasis mine)

35

- Don't expect to bring in a harvest when you haven't planted a seed
- Justice: lawfulness and morality
  - Includes discernment of right and wrong
- Like begets like
  - Including the power of the mind and emotions (Law of Attraction)
  - Power of words and thoughts, or focus
- Integrity and Ethics
  - Be honorable and don't be a schmuck
- Fairness (equitability, not showing preference or prejudice)
- Reciprocity (the urge to return favors or pay back when we've received, aka "trading")
  - For instance, if you're a coach desiring clients, invest in a coach yourself.
- Gratitude (rather than acting entitled)
- Decisiveness (let your Yes be Yes and your No be No)
- Optimism (the glass is the perfect size because you can always get a refill)
- Humility (be at peace with not having to prove yourself. Just be.)
- Being Intentional and Expectant (Faith and Hope)
  - Dream a bigger dream and believe it will come true
- Abundance and Generosity in mindset, worldview and actions
  - Opposite of lack and poverty
  - The pie is always big enough to serve everyone
- Forgiveness
  - Unforgiveness is the quickest way to set up blocks and limits to your success, as well as create dis-ease in your body

- Law of Promotion (Excellence)
  - Walk worthy of your calling, working for a higher purpose
  - Stewarding well to multiply resources and profits
- Speed of Implementation
  - Be quick to obey (starting and stopping)
  - As soon as you get a NOW download— ACTIVATE it

...and one of my favorites:

- Surprise and Delight your clients
  - Go the extra mile—above and beyond people's expectations
  - Stand out and be different

CHAPTER 4

YOUR BUSINESS DESTINY SCROLL

Just like your personal destiny scroll, the scroll or book of destiny for your business also exists in the spirit realm.

Not that long ago I discovered that I had been holding a counterfeit destiny belief. This is the shiny, impressive dream that looks good to the world...the kind you can explain to your family and friends. It makes sense. It makes you look good—successful. You can hang your identity on it.

God says He knew you and chose you before the foundations of the earth. (See Jer. 1:5, Ps. 139:16) He knew the mission you would be on, the trials you would face, the career path you would choose, and the people whose lives you would touch. He designed you for your destiny. Your destiny includes the unique destiny of your business, which is much bigger than you. It includes all the lives you will touch, and is interconnected with all of their destinies as well. Science proves this with the law of quantum entanglement. Whoa. That's a LOT to think about.

But back to my story. My internship to complete my bachelor's degree in interior architecture was a paid position with the Dept. of Veterans Affairs (VA). Right out of the gate I was making more money than my peers, and hadn't even graduated yet. Over the next 6 years I received 5 promotions, and my budget went from $5,000 to $1.2M per year . By the time I left the corporate realm for good in 2009, I had worked on multi-million dollar construction projects, been personally responsible for a $3.2M annual budget, and successfully managed up to 34 construction projects at one time. I proved myself an excellent steward of large amounts of money, including negotiating deals, and being able to handle hiring and leading teams. I was highly efficient, effective and organized. And stressed. And overweight. And divorced.

This was not what Father had planned. I had either been chasing a counterfeit destiny, or going after my destiny with my head/intellect (soul) instead of my heart/passion (spirit)...or a little of both.

What Business Truly is From a Spiritual Perspective.

When we establish a Kingdom business here on earth, in the spirit realm this looks like an act of war to the enemy. The earthly purpose is to bring solutions to problems, to gain market share and influence, and to increase wealth so you can do good—to leave a legacy. Well, who is the author of problems? Satan. Who wants all the power, control and wealth for himself? Satan. Your business is a vehicle to execute transformation from bad to good, in general. Who wants to keep things 'bad'? Satan. (Forgive me for sounding like the church lady from Saturday Night Live. LOL)

In the spirit realm, this vehicle looks like a weapon being built and deployed. You want to bring order to chaos, peace to turmoil, clarity to confusion, and a host of other Kingdom principles. You want to gain wealth to fund setting captives free and building the Kingdom. This does not make demons happy campers, and they will do whatever they can to destroy the business, or your ability to operate it effectively.

As in my counterfeit destiny example, Satan will lure you down the wrong path—or the right path for the wrong reasons—with the things you think will make you happy. You won't even realize you're in a war until you see the casualties...and maybe even then, in retrospect.

This is a WAKE UP situation!

Not necessarily for you, as you've already picked up this book. But please help get the word out to your Kingdom loved ones, friends and colleagues that doing business that builds God's Kingdom is a declaration of war, and they need to be prepared. You don't want to be the lone soldier who decided to invade Afghanistan by yourself!

"If you solicit good advice, then your plans will succeed. So don't charge into battle without wisdom, for wars are won by skillful strategy." —Prov. 20:18 (TPT)

One of the world-changers I have the privilege of working with shared with me how incredibly blessed she is to have received the scroll for her business. Shelley says that before she took the time to sit with the Lord and envision and co-create what she truly desires her business to be, it was like she was operating blind. She had no idea what the business was supposed to look like, no template. She was "perishing because of lack of vision."

"Break open your word within me until revelation-light shines out! Those with open hearts are given insight into your plans."

—Ps. 119:130 (TPT)

"The lenses of our past and our present circumstances blur the vision of our future."

—Dr. Faisal Malick

The vision the Lord gave her was like "Candyland" with a bouncy house and lemon and honey drops. This was to be the flavor and tone of her businesstry. She heard children laughing which meant her work was not to be tough and slogging it out—it would be playful and joy-filled! She now feels sunshine on her business and no longer feels like it's a prison. Now that she has the destiny scroll and vision for her business, Shelley is empowered and in her own lane where she feels comfortable, light and free! And her coaching calendar is fully booked. Yay God!

Receiving Your Destiny Scroll

Receiving the destiny scroll, or book, for your business is very similar to receiving your life destiny scroll. In my experience, and anecdotally, many people just receive their destiny scroll when they ask Yeshua or Yahweh for it, and don't necessarily have a sense of where they are in the heavenly realms. Some people report they were in a garden with the Lord, or they actually go or are led to the Hall of Records where, presumably, the scrolls and books are kept.

Because this is specific to business, I've discovered through my Business Ekkelsia group and working with clients, that we can go directly into the business center in heaven, and from there into the Court of Business and Finance to get the destiny scrolls needed. From my experience—yours may be different, and that's okay—the Court of Titles and Deeds is within the Court of Business and Finance. Again, it doesn't matter what heaven looks like to you, or even if you don't perceive a specific place at all. There is no wrong way to get your scroll. What matters is that you receive it, by faith if you have to, and you then engage with it to the best of your ability. The reason I'm explaining each step with visual cues is because I've found it helpful for the world-changers I work with. (And everyone I work with is changing the world in some way!)

Reading the process may not float your boat when it comes to actually doing it, so I've created a free downloadable guided activation for your convenience. Grab it here: SpiritCenteredBusiness.com/businessdestinybook. And for those of you who want the step-by-step checklist, zoom ahead a few pages, it's there.

Now, potentially you may have already received it as far as Heaven is concerned, but this exercise will solidify it for you, so go ahead and do it anyway. Use your imagination to start out if you're not a seasoned "heaven walker".

Start by grabbing your journal or a recording device, and sitting comfortably upright in a quiet place, free of sound and movement distractions...but not in bed. Close your eyes, relax and calm your body. I find that one somatic breathing cycle helps to get my body still. (10 deep medium-paced breaths with equal inhalation and exhalation, then 10 deep slower breaths with elongated exhalations.) If you get distracted, gently pull your focus back to the exercise, give yourself grace, and continue.

Pray this Opening/Covering Prayer
(aloud if possible)

Father God, I thank you for life and breath, and for loving me enough to create an amazing, hope-filled plan for my future. I ask for an open heaven all around me right now, and I call my spirit forward to connect with my Creator. I ask for a protective barrier around me that expands across time and space so that nothing outside of God's plans and purposes for me will be allowed to interfere or distract me. I declare I'm operating in stealth mode, undetectable by the enemy. Thank you Jesus, for tearing the veil between the dimensions and I step through you as the only door with access to Father's Kingdom. Holy Spirit, please open the eyes and ears of my heart, open my ability to perceive, and don't let me miss anything of what's going on in the spirit realm around me. I trust that I will receive the destiny scroll for my business today, regardless of whether or not I can see or read it. I trust the process by an act of my will. In the loving name of Jesus, Amen.

Step into the business center. I'll describe my perception of it, and it's perfectly fine if you don't see it this way. Just relax and see/perceive it the way you do. It's all good.

So, for reference—for you map-lovers like me—I've understood the Business Center to be on one of the sides of a large courtyard. On the other sides are the Justice Center where all the courtrooms and legal chambers are, and the Arts and Entertainment Center of Creativity. I don't have a solid understanding of what's on the other side or sides at this point, as I've never been there, or asked. Again, don't worry if you've seen it differently or heard the complexes called by other names. We're all doing our best and no one has the definitive "right" answer. I also suspect that our experience of heaven is subjective. God tends to speak to us in ways unique and personal. He loves us that much!

Back to stepping into the business complex. The lobby is a big room with a very high ceiling 50 feet tall or more, like an airport or hotel lobby. There are pleasant seating areas around to the sides, and directly in front of us is the horseshoe or half circle shaped help desk. There are attendants there and on the far side of the room behind the desk you can see the entrance to the atrium. There are lush green tropical gardens with pathways, water features, gazebos and benches. At the far end is the towering waterfall. But from this place standing in front of the help desk we can barely hear the waterfall because it's pretty far away. I've found that heaven expands and contracts as we need it and as we move through it. It changes, and it's all good. All of the office suites have a view of the atrium from whatever floor they are on. As a business owner, when you get your Declaration of Trade approved and receive your Deed of Commerce and Trade, that is your office suite—your trading floor.

If this is new to you, your Declaration of Trade is your partnership agreement with Heaven. It allows you to properly establish your business in Yahweh's Kingdom so you can access resources, protection, assistance and more. It also sets the expectations of how your business will operate, the culture, standards, and guardrails you will cultivate and maintain...which are all included in its destiny. The Lord showed me 1 Samuel 10:25 as a reference to drawing up this legal constitution-style document.

I want to encourage you, especially if you're new to exercising your imagination to step into the heavenly realms, that if you can be disciplined to come back to the same place and see it the same way, it will help you in your consistency and continuity and the reality of Heaven. This is a real place in Father's Kingdom. Which is another reason why I describe the business complex the same way for my clients as well. For consistency and for the ease of stepping into the spirit realm it's better to see it the same way each time. Just like our daily 3D lives—when we step into our house it looks the same, it doesn't change. The rooms are in the same position with the same furniture.

Back to getting your scroll. We're at the help desk and now you'll want to check in. We always want to honor protocol, especially if you're a guest, but even if you're a Son and new here. They usually have a clipboard and you just sign in with your name and your purpose for being here. Maybe you'll see an attendant there and you can just say this to them. State your purpose to receive your destiny scroll for your business. They will be happy you're there, and very helpful! You may be given a lanyard or a badge or something like that.

Next you will be escorted, or you can ask to be escorted, to the Court of Business and Finance, which in my experience has been across the lobby to the right. You'll leave the help desk behind and walk across the room and into a large corridor. For reference, the business library is also down this corridor, should you need it in the future. When you get to the large wooden double doors, your escort or Jesus will open them for you (or they'll just open— everything is very welcoming and inviting here!)

When you walk in through the doors, to your right is a wall full of pigeon holes that are about a foot or so square where all of the destiny scrolls or books are. There's a very impressive wall of them floor to ceiling. On the left are wooden seats, like a gallery. Sometimes there might be angels or other people there, especially if they're already on assignment for your business. They may come and watch the proceedings, so I like to be quiet for a minute and take a look and see if anyone's there. If you do see someone you can ask them if they're there for you. If so, you can invite them to help you receive and read your scroll. Find out what role they have in your business. Often, a person in white linen from the cloud of witnesses (see Heb 12:1) will be assigned as your main business advisor. When you get your Declaration of Trade approved you usually meet them, but they could show up now as well.

Walk into the room, and turn toward the scroll wall. Directly in front of you is the slightly raised magistrate's desk and in front of that desk is a table. Ask the attending angels to bring the destiny scroll or book for your business over to you and put it in your hands or it across your arms. Just be patient and see what happens. One client of mine "received" his scroll when the angels wrapped a belt of gold light around him. If you're a gadget person, you may receive a device that contains it. Don't discount anything, and ask questions if you need clarification or confirmation.

Be sure to treat everyone with respect and honor. Thank the magistrate and angels, or whomever is helping you. Just like you would here in the physical realm.

Read Your Scroll by Engaging It

First, just look at the scroll, or whatever you received. How does it feel? Is it weighty? Can you feel it in your hands? If it's a book, is it hard? Is it big, or small? What is it made of? If it's a scroll, is it one scroll all rolled up or is it like one paper rolled from both ends so it looks like two scrolls? Does it have handles? Or maybe your destiny scroll is in a case. I've had scrolls given to me that were in beautiful silver filigree boxes with gemstones on them. I've had some that just look like a piece of parchment paper tied with a ribbon. What color ribbon? If it's a device, what does it look like? How do you open it? Some open into a 3D hologram. Feel free to use the table in front of you. That's what it's for.

Write in your journal what your destiny scroll looks like and how it feels. Describe it in as much detail as you can. Each descriptor could be a clue as to what's inside! Later, when you're engaging with it you may want to come back to what you wrote to ask questions as to what it means. Such as, why does my scroll look like a book with a wooden cover?

Next I want you to look at the condition that it's in. Is it brand new? Like how a fresh book smells right off the printer and the paper is just so crisp. Is it brand new like it's never been engaged with before or does it have a little bit of age to it? Is it ancient? Maybe it's been waiting for you since the beginning of time! Who knows? Maybe it's only ancient as far back as your bloodline started to be entrepreneurs. It could be anything. Is it dusty, or deteriorating and falling apart and you need to clean it up or revive it? It could be burned or torn or shriveled and moldy. It could be in any condition for whatever reason we'll get to, so don't discount anything unusual you notice. Many people notice it feels alive, sentient. Yep—that happens!

If you do have something that's not quite right with it, don't worry. You can ask about why that happened later. Let's take care of it right now. If you haven't already, put the destiny scroll on the table and we're going to pour living water over it regardless of its condition. (see John 7:38, Rev. 7:17) I love this part! It reminds me of one of those capsules when I was a kid and we put this tiny little capsule into a cup of water and it opened up to be a sponge animal. Remember those? When you put living water on the scroll it will flesh out and get bigger and more robust, smoothing out wrinkles and healing and repairing all of the damage. All the dust and mold will go away and it's quite amazing to

"Write the vision and
make it plain on tablets,
that he may run who reads it."

—Habakkuk 2:2

Who needs to run with your vision? You do!

see. Even seemingly "perfect" scrolls or holograms will become weightier, brighter, more...present somehow.

Whatever happens for you when you do this, go ahead and write it down so that you can engage your scroll on a regular basis. Get to know your scroll and become really familiar with it. Things in heaven are often "alive". So it's perfectly fine to see and treat your scroll as a living being.

Now let's assume that your scroll is healthy and ready to be opened, and you have a "go-ahead". You can unroll it, take it out of the box or undo the ribbon or whatever needs to happen. You might need a key to unlock it, so you can just ask Jesus, the angels or attendants if they would please give you a key. If you have a device, maybe there's some sort of a chip that you need to put into a hologram that will fire it up, turn it on, or whatever. Just flow with whatever is going on for you.

My favorite way to begin the process of reading it is to step right into it. Now for someone who sees things literally, you'll be standing in the middle of that table about thigh high. For some, maybe the scroll came to life around you and now you're in an IMAX theater with screens all around you. Sometimes it will come to life like a hologram and it will literally be 3D around you. You can see things in dimensional form that you could interact with, such as a chair you could sit in. However it is for you, go with it. Make it as real as possible. You may hear things, or even smell or taste things!

If you do smell something or you hear talking, music or singing or there's something else going on be sure to ask about it. Be like a kid and continuously ask why! Then write down anything you're sensing as the answer, or if a memory comes to mind, see if you can draw the parallel. What is Heaven telling you?

Even though this note may go more with Destiny Mapping, it's worth mentioning here. Sometimes, especially with prolific seers, you'll see multiple scenes or snapshots at once or in quick succession. Don't panic. Just write down what you can catch, or track with them first, and then write them down, or record yourself or whatever. Because our scroll exists outside of time, sometimes you see things out of order or all at the same time. (Time is here in our 3D world to help us so everything doesn't all happen at once. Talk about chaos!) If you do experience your scroll this way, you'll need to sort it out by asking questions or looking for continuity clues. We'll talk more about this in the mapping section.

Envision Your Ideal Destiny

This exercise is a co-creating blend of you imagining or envisioning your desires while you're in heaven paying attention to what's going on and asking questions. This is you operating multi-dimensionally in the quantum realm of infinite possibilities, in God's Kingdom, and in the three dimensional realm of your physical existence. How cool is that!

That said, this is just one exercise you can do to "read" your scroll. Don't expect to be able to see it all at once, or to see a clear path from A to Z. In my experience, my rockstar clients unfold and discover pieces of their scroll over time as we work on issues that come up, or launching projects together. Many times we have to get something out of the way in order to see the next step, or to move the needle in our business.

In October of 2022 Beata from Kenya was facing stagnation in her business, and lack of stamina in her body. We had to remove lies about her identity, worthiness and capacity to handle things that had been planted in her father's life that were still resonating in her DNA. Once we did that she was able to look again at the truth of her destiny. She saw herself sitting on a crystal white throne next to Yahweh. She was given an hourglass like a snow globe filled with butterflies, fairies and snow! We asked what this meant, and she declared, "I have the ability to confidently create a beautiful world." She felt free and invigorated! The very next day she messaged me:

"I had an Amazing day today! I felt fully in charge, and we had the best sales we have ever had since March 2020."

—Beata M.

Yay God! Miracles are possible for you too. The first step in creating them is to know what you truly desire.

Psalms 37:4 says, "Delight yourself also in the Lord and He will give you the desires of your heart." He will put His desires into you, but YOU still have to do the desiring. It's not God's job to do it for you. Take this visioning exercise seriously...and have fun!

Now that you've stepped into your open scroll, just look around and see what you see. This represents a snapshot in time in your business. Dial the timeline to a future date so you can see what the ideal future of this business looks like. Ask the angels to help you if you need it. This is your vision for this business. What would it look like? Feel free to use your imagination as far as desires and preferences because you are a creator just like the Creator who made you. Take a look around at the room you're in: an office at your desk, a conference room, a salon, a studio, working from your backyard near the swimming pool, wherever represents your typical day at "the office", wherever that happens to be for you.

In the next few pages I'm going to throw out a lot of ideas to give you an idea of how detailed you should make your vision. When you actually do the exercise you get to draw your own picture. Don't let my leading lead you astray.

Okay, let's assume you're in your office with an amazing view. What does the view look like? Are you in a big city such as New York? Are you in the mountains? In a small town? In a beach community? What's on your desk? Do you have a calendar there? A phone? A computer? Do you have pictures of family or friends? What other furniture is in the room? Do you have a fireplace? A seating area? A conference table?

Look on the wall. Do you have a picture or artwork, or certificates or diplomas or any other mementos of your accomplishments? Maybe there's a picture of you with a person of influence in your industry that you always wanted to meet. Now you've met them and maybe even have a relationship with them. What does that mean to you?

Now sit down in your chair. What kind of chair is it? What does it feel like? What color is it? What material? What does the room look like from this point of view? What's across the room in front of you? What's behind you? A credenza? A bookcase?

Really engage with this picture to give it vivid details. How do you feel in this space? Connect your body to this vision in your mind, which is the spirit realm. Feel the joy, satisfaction, pride of accomplishment, peace, certainty, the confidence of "it is already here". Write down all the details, and how you feel.

Now think about how you want to spend your ideal business/working day from this place. Remember that you get to decide how you want to spend your day. If you say, "Well it's up to God." Well guess what? He gave you stewardship of your business and it is not up to Him to do your desiring for you. You are engaging the destiny scroll He planned for you, but not every detail is there. He doesn't want to stifle your creativity...He wants to see what you'll do with it. You have to make the decision on what you want, and then hold that desire until it manifests. (More on this later, I don't want to break the flow.)

So what would be your perfect ideal day? How would you get up in the morning? Out of a huge king-sized bed with a fluffy down comforter in a big sun-filled bedroom? Or your favorite cozy little nook that you love to sleep in?

And then what happens? Who will you spend the morning with? Do you eat breakfast? Workout? Go for a walk? Then when you come into your office, who are you spending your day with there? Who are your ideal clients? Picture your ideal client walking in right now, or coming online if you're Zooming. Who are they? Are they male or female? Who do you really want to play in the sandbox with? There's no wrong answer, just choose. How old are they? What are they wearing? What socioeconomic status do they have? Are they similar to you, or are they different from you?

Let's keep going. You need this info for your Declaration of Trade and for your physical world marketing, so let's stick with it as long as we're here. Where do they live? Do they live in a gated community? Do they live in an apartment? What kind of car do they drive? That also speaks to their psychographics. What thrills them? What turns them on? Just write these things down about your ideal client who just came in. I really want you to get to know who you are called to serve. They are part of your destiny, and it's right there in your scroll.

Who is on the other side of you building this business? Who are you making trades with? The better you can describe them, understand them, and speak their language, the better your marketing will be. So the better you will be able to serve them and fulfill the destiny of your business. They just showed up in your office, either physically or online, with a problem for which they believe you have the solution.

So now let's really look at the exact problem or set of problems you solve. So many business owners get this wrong, or can't define it. Usually when I ask people what problem they solve, they tell me what solution they bring. This is understandable, don't get me wrong. Our solutions are very familiar to us. This is what you love to do and what you're really good at.

But in order to really connect with your dream client, you have to focus on them, not you. Really step into their shoes and see the problem from their point of view. What are they thinking? What are they feeling? What do they fear? What do they want instead? What are their hopes and dreams and desires? What solutions have they already tried? What emotional state are they in when they come to you? The better you can articulate their problem, the more they will automatically and subconsciously believe you have the solution. This is what will make your branding and marketing magnetic!

Let's get really specific, and take a really simple example. Say you're selling drills. Their problem is not that they want to buy a drill. The problem is they want to make a hole, and a drill will solve the problem. You have to know about the problem in order to sell them the right drill. What size hole do they need? What kind of material are they going through? Think ahead to a problem they may not even know they have or will have. Will they need to screw something in? Would they also like to use the drill as a screwdriver?

These kinds of questions are going to be on the Declaration of Trade, so as you're standing here in your destiny scroll with assistants around to help, I would definitely go ahead and get the answers. Especially while you're in a flow. You can always revisit your scroll, of course, if answers aren't coming, or you need more in the future.

Remember, if your mind drifts while you're waiting for answers, gently pull it back to the scene. Take a deep breath to recenter your focus, and continue.

Moving on. Take a look at your calendar. Whether it's digital or paper or however you keep a calendar, take a look at how often you are working. How many hours a week, or hours a day, or how many days a month? What does your ideal calendar look like?

At this point, you've written down what your dream office looks like, and who your dream client is, including the exact problem they have. You've thought about how you want to spend your day and the amount you want to work on or in your business. How do you feel? Getting this clarity and focus on your future should feel freeing and exhilarating! Are you excited to manifest this destiny in your 3D experience? Generating and holding the emotion of this moment is the key to bringing it into your now. Dial up the

"The key to manifesting your miracle lies in proactively governing your emotions and harnessing their power to intentionally create your world."

—Virginia Killingsworth

emotions—feel them in your body. Joy, satisfaction, pride of accomplishment, wonder—that "pinch me, it's gotta be God!" feeling. You are literally rewiring your brain to attract and create this future!

Before you leave this place in heaven, I invite you to ask any other questions you may have. Jesus is there with you, and I guarantee there are beings who are assigned to your destiny scroll there too. Take a quiet moment and see if any other questions come up for you to get more clarity on. Write down the answers, and be sure to note the questions too, if they are not answered in this engagement.

When you feel you are finished, ask that your scroll be closed again. Put it into your inner being. Just make a prophetic gesture of putting it inside you so it's locked up. I'm going to pray for you.

I bless you with everything you envisioned. Holy Spirit, please seal it across all timelines, all dimensions, and across all realms. I ask that all portals, gateways, interface points and bridges are guarded and protected so that your destiny scroll is completely safe. I declare that it cannot be hijacked, lost, stolen, abandoned, traded away, or deteriorated. Angels, I ask that you help keep that scroll safe because the enemy wants to kill, steal and destroy their hopes and dreams and their business. I declare the enemy has no access, and that the manifestation of this scroll, this destiny, and this future would be accelerated instead. I ask for a boldness to wash over them now, a confidence of knowing You have a good plan for them and their business. Father, we trust you. It is finished! I ask for an oil of ease to be poured out over them as they continue to engage with their scroll until they see it come to pass in the earth. Thank you, Father God. Thank you for this time.

I pray all of this in the mighty and wonderful name of Yeshua Hamashiach, our Lord and Savior. Amen.

Thank the angels and everyone else helping you. Bless them and return your focus to your physical environment— holding on to the emotions. That brings Heaven to earth. Your brain and body don't know the difference between a spiritual event and a "real" one. That's why I recommend engaging in a meditation like this where you step into your ideal future and generate those emotions as often as possible. Doing it daily or both morning and night will accelerate it manifesting on the earth.

It will also be critical for you to shut down any negative thoughts or feelings about your future, or the reality, or "success" of this exercise. That's like having one foot on the gas and one on the brakes at the same time. You'll just spin your wheels. It's a discipline...and **your destiny is worth your discipline!**

If you just read this through and didn't actually engage, I HIGHLY encourage you to set aside time to do the work. You picked up this book for a reason. You want to know if you're on the right track with your business, and this exercise will give you clarity and confirmation one way or the other. Pray and press in!

Do it now!

If you prefer to listen to this as a guided activation, you may download it at SpiritCenteredBusiness.com/business-destinybook.

I believe in you, and I believe that Father gave you this destiny scroll for a reason. You have what it takes to fulfill it. He designed you for it. You have even more inside you than you think you do. We all do. You are bigger on the inside than you ever could imagine!

Receiving and Reading Your Destiny Scroll Checklist

1. Get comfy and relaxed in a quiet, distraction-free space with your journal
2. Pray: Acknowledge your Creator and ask for a spirit-to-spirit encounter, turning your attention to Jesus as the only door.
3. Protect this time from any evil influence or distraction.
4. Envision yourself walking up to the business center help desk and checking in.
5. Proceed to the Court of Business and Finance as you are led.
6. Ask to enter the Court of Titles and Deeds.
7. Ask for your business destiny scroll/book to be brought to you.
8. Engage it: Open it or have it opened, and "read it".
9. Write out the vision of what your business is to be in as much vivid detail and emotionally charged language as possible.
10. Watch for the unfolding of it, or what's trying to happen in your physical realm in the next days, weeks or months. Pay attention and look for clues! Remember that a seedling does not look like a full grown tree. There's a process to get to your ideal vision.
11. Set aside regular times to engage with it often, especially as you need to make decisions.
12. BONUS: Do Destiny Mapping to plan your year, quarter, or even week, as desired.

Tips on "Seeing/Reading or Engaging" Your Destiny Scroll

There are essentially three ways to know what's on your destiny scroll. The first way, outlined above, I call "co-creating". The second way, most often used in stewarding your destiny as discussed in chapter 5, can be called "manifesting". It's holding the expectation of what you're intending by an act of your will—which is faith—and eagerly watching for clues to what is unfolding...which almost never looks like we thought it would. Don't miss a forward step because you didn't recognize it. Be open to possibilities.

The third way is "standing". After you've done all else, just stand in childlike expectation, trusting in God's promises that no matter what your circumstances look like, He has a good plan and it will come to pass. All three take discipline; consistent focus of intention and maintaining your emotional state.

1. Don't try to parse out if this is just you making stuff up, or if it's actually happening in the spirit realm. Relax and hold peace about the process. As long as you've done the protocols above, just Trust.

2. Ask questions. Question everything you're perceiving, however you're experiencing it. Then quietly wait for answers, or shifts in the "picture". Such as, "Why am I seeing swirling purple? (wait) What does it mean? (wait) Does it represent something?" (wait)

    If you see a series of things, ask how they go together. What are you trying to show me here? Stay in a possibilities mindset. Afterall—the quantum realm is the place of infinite possibilities.

3. If you're getting distracted and not able to focus, just stop. Take a walk, a drink of water, go do something else and come back to it. There's no rush, and striving only narrows your connection pathway. Focusing on God in peace and serenity opens it up. Curiosity and wonder (like a child) help too!

4. You have the right of refusal. God won't override your free will. If you see something on your scroll you really don't want to do, ask why it's there. You may be being called into a new assignment you hadn't thought of before, so it seems "off". Stay calm. Take time (days and weeks—not minutes) to meditate on it, meaning noodling it over in your mind. Ask God about it. Think of the what ifs. And know that you can say, "No, I don't want this assignment." Maybe it will come back around...maybe not. The point is, God's plan can accommodate your issues or desires or phobias, or whatever—and it will still be a good plan. He still loves you and wants you to succeed wildly!

5. What to do if there's just nothingness. There may be bondages that keep you from seeing. There may be deeper roots that need to be pulled out, but here's the quick fix to try first. Name whatever it is: Blankness, Blackness, Nothingness, etc. Say, "Blackness, what right do you have to be here?" Listen/feel for an answer. You may hear a word such as "unforgiveness" or "doubt" or "anger", or you may feel resentment or some other negative emotion. Name the emotion or say the word you heard, and ask Jesus to forgive you for coming into agreement with it. Say out loud that you break agreement with it. Give it to Jesus. Receive your

forgiveness. Declare yourself forgiven and free. And look again. Usually this opens your ability to connect, but it could also take a few rounds if there are layered obstacles blocking you. If you need help, I'm available. Book a Liebust session with me here: SpiritCenteredBusiness.com/healing

CHAPTER 5

YOUR DESTINY IS WORTH YOUR DISCIPLINE

Stewarding Your Destiny

"Co-creating your future and manifesting your destiny means watching for clues of it happening, while intentionally holding the joy and exhilaration of it already having happened."

— Bralynn Newby

It's YOUR responsibility to bring the blueprint from heaven to the earth. You need to build it. You need to incubate it in prayer and emotionally charged meditation. You need to be consistent with holding the vision and speaking the declarations. Remember that you only saw one snapshot of a fully mature business. The majority of your destiny scroll—the path of its maturing, hasn't been written yet. The outline is there, but when you're ready, the

"Faith and doubt will always exist together. Believing is choosing faith over doubt."

—Dr. David Yonggi Cho

Lord will give you the pen to co-create the details. SO EXCITING! This also allows for detours (positive or negative) and spins on the hamster wheel (lesson learning do-overs). Remember the "Family Circus" cartoon where the kid would wander all over the neighborhood on his way home? That's what our life journey is like. Enjoy it! Who wants to just go straight home anyway? LOL

As you think about what the future of your business looks like, hold the intention in your heart that it is manifesting on earth. Holding that expectant hope and faith, and staying in gratitude creates forward movement that shepherds, nurtures and protects it. This is like a hen brooding over her eggs. Our Creator brooded over the waters of the deep as He was creating our world. (see Gen 1:2)

If we're looking at this scientifically, there's a frequency, a vibrational sound component to creation as well. This is why Yahweh released His voice—his signature sound frequency, and said, "Let there be light." Being made in His image, our voice is our unique frequency as well. Not to get too far into the weeds here on quantum science or the power of our words, but it's true. Our thoughts and words are real things, and make a real difference. The power of life and death are in the tongue. (see Prov 18:21) Which is why a shift in your circumstances requires a shift in your thinking, a shift in your dominant emotional state, and a shift in the words you speak. You must demonstrate your belief that it is already done by speaking and acting as if it were.

Salome, one of my world-changing clients in South Africa, had a history of opportunities falling through just as she reached the threshold of stepping into them. We asked Jesus to show her what was in the threshold of a current opportunity that was keeping her in this pattern. There was a scorpion there that had a legal right to hang out because she was coming into agreement with unworthiness. We broke that off and she started declaring the truth of her expertise and calling, and who God says she is. I also gave her the assignment of writing out the vision of the fullness of that opportunity—her dream job—looked like and felt like. That night she stirred up her emotional state into the "it-is-finished" frequency of joy and gratitude and excitement of having already landed this job. At 8:00 the next morning the company called and said they wanted her on board! Yay God!

Of course, these quick co-creating miracles are amazing and fun...but the real test is when you have to steward the dream over time without wavering.

"You should have a burning desire for a goal, and you must **keep on** *seeing that goal accomplished."*

—Dr. David Yonggi Cho

The problem most people run into is that they renegotiate. When a goal or dream doesn't happen right away there's a tendency to get into doubt and fear. If we let those two hooligans run free in our mind, the slippery slope will have us choosing to believe a less-than-God's-best outcome. Pretty soon we're all the way back down to settling for the "safe" comfort zone of our current circumstances. Back to drifting in default mode. Most people let go of their dreams at the first obstacle. But you're not most people! You picked up this book because you know God has a bigger plan for your life! I'm here to cheer you on to build the muscle of stick-to-it-ness. Just like weight training, the more resistance, the bigger and stronger the muscle. Look at you go, Arnold! LOL

Another stumbling block that can trip us all up is that we believe we have a plan from God—we've prayed over it, researched, gotten confirmation, the whole nine yards...and then it flops. We would have the tendency to think we missed God, we didn't hear right. But the truth may be that that "failure" was a necessary step on the way to your destiny. There were lessons you had to learn, people you had to meet, wounds you had to heal. Growth and expansion seasons aren't always pretty...and they're often quite ghastly. It's a good idea to ask if you made assumptions that were incorrect so you don't repeat them. But once you have peace again about the bigger picture, just keep trusting Yahweh's good plan. Forgive yourself. Say, "Well, THAT happened," and move on. Ask for the next step forward.

"When things go wrong, don't go with them."

—Elvis Presley

Hold onto your dream with a fierce tenacity no matter what the peanut gallery in your head chatters to you. No matter what your past would dictate. No matter what your neighbors or friends or family say. No matter what your current circumstances look like. You just keep doing YOU— the bigger, bolder, more authentic, more alive you you are destined to be. You can literally build new neural pathways in your brain in just 21 days if you doggedly visualize and speak and believe. Your old pathways (patterns of behavior) will dissolve if you refuse to use them. Just like a path through the grass.

What you DO need to let go of is the "how".

Here's an instance where I didn't even think for a moment about the how...I didn't even think about "when." I was

"...plan your life around the noblest way to benefit others."

—Rom. 12:17b (TPT)

making plans to attend a conference in another state. The last time I had been with that group was when I was one of the speakers. I missed speaking. I'd been out of it for a few years, and then the 2020 dupery happened. But I saw myself on stage again, speaking to a large hotel conference room full of people who loved what I shared. My vision was strong and bold, in a posture of leadership and camaraderie. The audience and I were having fun! With a sense of eager anticipation I said, "Okay, Lord, I'm ready to do that again." And I let it go. Two weeks before the conference the organizer said a speaker dropped out and asked if I wanted to speak. I said YES, of course...and then thought, "Oh dirt. What the heck am I going to speak on???" LOL It turned into a terrific opportunity to be the "opening act" for Ian Clayton, so the room was full, and I was in my element! I did hold a posture of bold leadership, and we did have fun!

We're about to go into destiny mapping a plan to get from where you are to where you want to be, but this is where you have to trust that God knows the best way for YOU...which may not be the best way for anyone else. Your path may include muscle-building failures. It's a statistical fact that people who succeed the most also fail the most. It's just part of the journey. He may also want to give you exceedingly abundantly above and beyond anything you could ever hope or dream! (see Eph 3:20) So hold your plan loosely while you hold your vision tightly.

Destiny Mapping

Someone smarter than me probably said something to this effect, I just don't know if I've heard it or not. So I'm just going to say it, "A life well lived is just the compounding effect of days well lived." Destiny mapping is simply planning to live each day well. Intentionally on purpose, yet in joy and freedom. The reason you want to do this is not to create an onerous burden, but to build an inner structure where the swirling vortex of indecision and stuckness and the temptations of Distractionland are minimized and exit routes are made ready.

You can create a visual map or a simple spreadsheet, whichever you prefer to give you a clear view of your destination and the milestones to guide you along the way. It's a high-level tool to keep you moving forward between the guardrails and help you off the merry-go-round when you need it.

Once you've received your destiny scroll and "read" it, or engaged with it as much as you can, and written out the vision (or 'A' vision) of it, it's time to make a plan—a roadmap to get you there.

> "Within your heart you can make plans for your future,
> but the Lord chooses the steps you take to get there."
>
> —Prov. 16:9 (TPT)

Prework

1. If you haven't already, write out your mandate, mission, and vision statement. You don't need to wordsmith it to marketing perfection, just get the pin in the map.
2. Properly establish your business in heaven with your Declaration of Trade and Deed of Commerce and Trade (see chapter 2 on Access). Grab the template for free on SpiritCenteredBusiness.com/

businessdestinybook. Or take the full course online—also on the website.

3. Make the decision and commitment that your destiny is worth your discipline. Why do all this work just to fall back into your default drifting position as soon as you're done reading this book?

I like to do as much as possible wholistically. So for each step of creating your destiny map, you could see where you are spiritually and in your soul as well. Are you feeling connected to your Source, and feeling His love and presence? Don't try to work out your spiritual muscles if you really need spiritual healing. What about the state of your soul; your mind, will and emotions? If you're going through or just coming out of big changes or trauma in your life, it's not the time to build. It's time to heal and rest. And regarding your physical world, do an inventory of your environment, what else is going on in your life that requires your time, energy and attention? Even look at your health and fitness. How is your energy level, or stamina?

Like the axiom, don't go grocery shopping when you're hungry...don't design a destiny map when another area of your life or your being is distracting or influencing you. There's a spiritual principle here I'd like to point out. When you design or build something in the physical world under pressure or in fear, doubt and unbelief—those frequencies get woven into the foundational fabric of the thing. I see this all the time when Liebusting businesses. Symptoms like stagnation, everything feeling like pushing through taffy, frustration, discord and malaise show up, usually rooted in the subconscious lies and accusations of its conception. That's why it's best to do this work in a joyful, expectant frame of mind. I bless you with one right now!

Also, know that your destiny map is a living document, subject to change along your route depending on various factors. My prayer for you is to design your business around the life you want to live so you get to work, rather than having your business controlling your life so you have to work.

Okay, assuming all systems are GO...let's get to it.

Step One: Determine Where You Are

The way I've experienced my destiny scroll and those of my clients is like a blueprint. It's a picture of the finished, built business in a moment of time. So we now need to create a roadmap to get from where you are to where you want to be—that blueprint. In order for your GPS to get you where you want to go, you must enter your starting point. In order to map the trajectory forward, you also need to take an inventory of where you've been.

Since I was a gun coach, let's use that analogy. In order to hit the target, you want to line your rear sight (back of the gun) up to the front sight (end of the barrel). You need those two points in order to hit the third one—the target. The rear sight in your destiny scroll is where you've been. Not the traumas and detours of life, but rather, your natural giftings, strengths and experiences that have made your heart come alive along the way. The front sight is where you are currently.

When shooting, your eye is focused on the front sight, so the rear sight and the target appear a little out of focus, but they are in the picture, and very important...obviously! We're going to do the same with your business.

Since I work with both new and established business owners, I'll give two different ways to establish your rear and front sights. You can choose which, or a combo, to use.

Just in case it needs to be said, you need to WRITE out the answers, preferably in your own hand (not typed), and not just think about them. Thoughts exist in the spirit realm, so you'll still be operating there if you don't pull them into the 3D realm by writing them out.

Established Business

You may wish to do this with your board or leadership team so everyone is on the same page and can contribute.

Let's do your front sight first. Do an inventory of your current KPIs (Key Performance Indicators) plus an inventory of current initiatives or projects. Write these down, pull up the spreadsheet, open the tracking or project management software, whatever. But I do want you to get your arms around everything going on in your business from a high level. Don't judge or analyze yet, just gather.

Make a list of ongoing operations.

Where have you allocated resources and personnel to accomplishing tasks?

What has already been planned, but not implemented?

What ideas are hovering, but yet to be planned out?

Now take a look at your rear sight—where you're been. Re-ground yourself in your big WHY. Why did you start this business in the first place? Do you have the same fire and passion as when you started? Completing your Dec of Trade will also give you this insight.

It's easy to so identify with your business and what it does that you lose sight of your own passion. This example may help you separate the two. When we started with Deb's passion, (the first item on the Dec of Trade), she said she was called to real estate to redeem the land and bring it back to its original purpose. Sounds good, right? But that's more of a mandate statement than a BIG WHY—a deep PASSION that ignites her and gets her going in the hard times. When we drilled down, we got closer to the fire with "I'm a waymaker, I bring light, I shift the atmospheres of rooms when I walk in, I work the room and make things happen." I asked if she's been that way since childhood, and she perked up and said, "Yes! I truly believed the world stopped when I wasn't there." SHAZAM—that's her passion! She makes the world go! Can you feel the juice on that?! It removes all striving, all performance, all perfectionism because the "work" happens because of who she is.

What is it that happens just by you being you? Effortless, invigorating, life-giving. Your "Chariots of Fire" moment where you can say you feel God's pleasure. Write it down.

Now let's do that for the company itself. What about its history is significant or compelling? Does it have its own watershed moment? What was/is its mission and values? (Assuming they passionately express your unique brand promise.) Also ask any other questions pertinent to your particular business that will pull the whole picture into view for you.

New or Not Yet Business
(Especially for Coaches—My Wheelhouse)

Let's do your rear sight first. Take a look back in your life and make a list of the stories that shaped you—that brought you to this moment on your timeline.

What experiences have you had that you can draw wisdom lessons from?

What mistakes have you made that you learned from and don't want to make again?

BIG NOTE: Don't ever be afraid to make mistakes! We all do, it's how we succeed. No judging or fear, just taking inventory. Making notes.

What passions of your past have given you the insight and courage to step into making money by serving with them?

Where have there been patterns of interest or enjoyment in your area of expertise?

What fuels you, fills you up and makes your heart come alive?

Now the front sight:

What's already trying to happen? Are divine connections coming into place, or opportunities opening up? What ideas are you currently exploring or working on fleshing out?

Reconnect to why you started or want to start this business. This is your BIG WHY from the Dec of Trade. It's usually a gap you see in the marketplace that solves a problem that either ticks you off or makes you cry.

Step Two: Sort and Analyze the Now

If your current inventory and parts of the vision get mixed up in steps two and three, that's okay. This is only ONE way to create a roadmap. You have freedom to go with the flow!

Established Business

Check your metrics. Are your KPIs really meaningful, and is tracking them actually effective?

Several times in my corporate career management would get a wild hair and have us spending time tracking and reporting on things that ended up falling by the wayside. Hundreds of hours of productivity were lost because the metrics they wanted were not meaningful, and the collection of the data was neither efficient nor effective. Don't be that guy. Just scrap the project and streamline your dashboard. What do you REALLY need to keep your eye on?

Have you lost your love? Are you still passionate about the solutions you bring to the world? Or is it time to make a shift?

Where can you trim fat and streamline? What projects have been hanging around that just need to be released back into the ether? Don't be afraid of archiving or pitching. A great idea will come back around if the timing wasn't right the first time. Purge the old to make room for the new. Ask: What can I say No to?

New or Not Yet Business

Do your best to determine the first or next step and focus only on that. I know—waaaaay easier said than done. Give yourself grace. But seriously, market research one thing, if that shows promise, test it, if that goes well, sell it, if people buy, build it. One thing. I know you want to solve everyone's problems, and you're multi-talented and multi-passionate. But multi-tasking does NOT work. It's fools gold. Make a decision and stick with it until you're sure it's no longer producing fruit, or you get a clear "Drop it" from heaven.

Remember, you can make one inch worth of progress in a hundred directions, or you can make a hundred inches of progress in one.

Use the Whole YOU: Spirit, Soul and Body

We are multidimensional beings, so I like to engage every aspect of myself in bringing my vision to life. I encourage you to do the same, even if you're just learning. It gets easier, I promise. For each step of this mapping process don't forget to ask the Lord for guidance. I usually have to put something together and ask, "Did I get this correct, yes or no."

Then check in with your soul. How do you really feel about this? Does it feel true for you, and not just something you thought would be good? A little nervousness is natural. See if you can determine where it's coming from—a truth, or a lie.

And, as I mentioned above, does this choice use Wisdom and Prudence in the 3D world with whatever else is going on in your life or in the world. Even if it doesn't make sense but you feel you've heard from Yahweh and you have a settled peace inside, go with it. Always be quick to obey.

Step Three: Sort and Analyze the Vision

Sometimes when we see or unpack the destiny scroll for our business it's like puzzle pieces dumped on a table. In the visioning exercise I had you put the puzzle pieces together as best you could, and add your imagination to complete the picture. During that you may have seen or perceived things that didn't seem to fit. Or when you go back to re-engage that may happen. From what I understand, because our scroll exists outside of time as we know it, we may need to sort the puzzle pieces not only by "thing", but also by time. When does this piece happen, not just what is it and where does it fit. Not everyone will have this issue, but we've come across it in coaching, so I thought I'd mention it. It's a matter of asking the question, "When does this piece go?" It might be next week, next month, or five years from now. Just do your best. Doing this mapping exercise will help.

For both established and new businesses, chunk the vision into the various areas of business.

So, the parts you may have written down in the vision could be:

- Team/Roles of others
- Vendors/suppliers
- Product offering
- Office space/environment
- Role you play (instead of the current wearer of all hats, you probably saw yourself as president or CEO)
- Things you spend time doing (You may have seen yourself traveling or hosting events, or whatever, which is different from your now.)
- (Anything else that comes to mind...)

For each piece of the vision decide:

1. Objective: What's your first or next step toward it?
2. Strategy: What do I need in order to do this? (How the objective will be met. Mindset shifts, training, connections, resources, etc.)
3. What would the next significant milestone be? (Plot as many milestones as you can.)

This draws your blueprint, or roadmap

Here's an example:

Let's say the vision is to have a well paid, fully staffed team. You need to decide which roles need to be filled in what order, and at what capacity.

1. Objective: Bring on a part-time virtual assistant to handle social media and some repetitive admin tasks, such as weekly content posting and emails.
2. Strategy: I need:
   a. $X monthly ($ per position and add them up)
   b. Each task ready to delegate: checklist of what needs to be done, and expectations of what "done" looks like.
   c. Research where to find the person I need.
   d. Contractor agreement with the working relationship outlined, including non-disclosures, intellectual property, and other parameters.
3. Next milestones would be:
   a. Bring on part-time producer for video and audio content
   b. Increase tasks and hours for my virtual assistant
   c. Bring on a part-time web tech
   d. Give 40 hrs/week worth of work to VA to make them full time, increase their rate
   e. Bring on a 2nd VA part-time with graphic design and copywriting skills
   f. ...and so on

Then do this process for each of the areas of business you have in your vision. There are several good "roadmap" tools if you wish to create a document/system you and your team can use and refer to together. My team and I use Trello with Google Drive.

You need to decide what works for you...always being flexible to change it up. You can get as detailed as you want here—but I would caution against spending so much time planning that you don't get to the doing. That's the third

"*Planning to Profit*" in my signature system...you've got to get out of the planning stage and into the profiting stage!

Don't skip planning, just don't hang out there. Stuck happens when you're starting with a blank slate or you've got so much detail that the first "well, THAT didn't work out the way I thought it would" (which happens all the time) throws you. Give yourself something to work with—but don't overwhelm yourself or paint yourself into a corner. Your future you will thank you!

Do this now!

(*And of course I'm available to help.*)

Guardrails

When you've mapped how you're going to get from where you are currently to your destiny, you just have to put guardrails in place to follow through with meditating and engaging your scroll on a regular basis. Use the prayers and declarations in Section 2 to anchor the quantum reality of your destiny already being done into the physical realm. We'll go over more of this in the *Daily Action Guide* section in the Conclusion.

CHAPTER 6

IMPACT

The last bit of training I want to address before we get to the actual prayers and declarations is how your health, family, environment, mindset, and so on affect your ability to execute your assignments and the impact your business has.

Energetic Forces to Manage

Everything is energy, or frequency, and energetic waves are all around us all the time. Unless we're in a faraday cage that blocks energy waves from the outside, we're constantly being bombarded with them. From electro-magnetic pulses from 5G, cell phones, radio and television, and so on, to your next door neighbor screaming at their kids.

Obviously you're in business to make an impact in the world, to create beauty, function, ease and flow and to bring solutions to problems. The more people you serve and profit you make, the more change you can create—the more Kingdom you can build. It's that whole "on earth as it is in heaven" thing.

So let's talk about a few things that have the potential to either block or limit your impact, or enhance and expand it.

The first is your health. The amount of impact you can have and legacy you leave, and even the extent to which you fulfill your destiny is intrinsically tied to the amount of energy and vitality you have. I know this from personal experience. I have been near-bedridden once in my career and twice in my business. All three instances pretty much wiped me out financially because I couldn't work. I was laid off of my job where my employer was also my insurer. My story certainly isn't unique, and I'm sure you get the picture. Moving on.

As I write this I'm getting more and more into biohacking longevity, even though I've been a fitness and fuel (nutrition) and mind/body science aficionado for years. But there's something to the new innovations that are coming out in regenerative medicine that the Lord is really highlighting to me as necessary for fulfilling our purpose on earth. I truly believe, like Einstein, that the future of medicine is frequency, and we need to embrace energy medicine. Those of us called to serve and build in a bigger way—and that's YOU because you're reading this book—are going to have to live longer with a longer healthspan in order to accomplish our mission. It's bigger than us!

A deep dive here is beyond the scope of this book, but since we've talked about frequency and quantum neuroscience in co-creating your future, just a simple tie-in is in order. We are energetic beings emanating electro-magnetic fields of energy that fluctuate with our emotional and physical state. Health and vitality are higher frequency states than sickness and lethargy. Food from the earth is higher frequency than processed frankenfoods.

To stay in high frequency or raise it, here are a few general tips. ...and am I perfect at all of them? Oh heck no...just for the record. ☺

1. Time restricted eating. Dr. David Sinclair is a Harvard Medical School professor in the Department of Genetics and co-director of the Paul F. Glenn Center for Biology of Aging Research, and author of the book Lifespan. He says the number one key to longevity is to eat less often.1 I started intermittent fasting in 2019, using a 14/10 ratio, meaning 14 hours off, and a 10 hour fueling window. At the end of 2022 I changed to a 16/8 plan, and frankly—it's so easy and so good for me that I often go 18/6. Guys, it's just not that hard. Skip breakfast and stop eating after dinner. My normal is: 1st meal at 12 or 1pm and done eating by 7 or 8pm. No calories before noon or after 8.

2. Move your body. We're not built to sit all day, yet our jobs often require it. Get up, get your blood flowing, stretch—do something throughout the day. I keep my rebounder handy for quick bounces between meetings. When I worked in an office I would go in the bathroom and do jumping jacks, and always took my phone callers for a walk. Beyond moving throughout the day, just 30 minutes of exercise 3-5 days per week elevates mood, improves cardio-vascular health, and improves strength and fitness and so much more. Not moving = death...in many more ways than you can imagine. Your destiny is worth your discipline. Just do it.

3. Drink water. Not soda, not coffee, not energy drinks...water. It lubricates everything in your body, makes muscles work, makes your brain function, makes your digestive system go (pun intended), and flushes toxins out. Drink at least ½ of your body weight in ounces every day. If you need to shed fat, drink more.

4. Get good sleep. Not getting enough REM sleep literally damages your brain. There are several sleep hacks available. This is one of my challenge areas, so I've tried almost all of them, and continually work at finding the best combo for whatever's going on in my body and environment. Dr. Andrew Huberman, Ph.D., is a neuroscientist and tenured professor in the department of neurobiology, psychiatry and behavioral sciences at Stanford School of Medicine. He has a great podcast with several episodes on sleep. Check out the Huberman Lab podcast on YouTube.2

5. Stop sugar. It's a toxin that's killing you. Just stop. Most frankenfoods have sugar disguised because it's addictive (even more than cocaine) and will keep you buying and eating more. It dumbs you down, makes you sick and lethargic, steals your creativity and motivation, and feeds disease...disease. Low frequency. Death. Do your research, be vigilant, find healthy alternatives and don't be fooled by deceptive labels or marketing. Such as: a cup (8 oz) of orange juice has as much sugar as a candy bar, yet is billed as a "health food". Don't buy the lie. Just say no.

Relationships Can Power You Up or Drain You

Be aware of people who habitually operate in low frequency (toxic) thoughts, behaviors and words. Try to minimize your exposure to them, if possible. If you need to be around them, do your best to bring the higher frequency emotional state so you can shift the atmosphere. Remember—the dominant frequency wins. Don't let their slime stick! Maybe you can encourage them to learn new coping skills and habits that will benefit you both.

Clear the Clutter

"If it doesn't add value to your life,
it doesn't belong in your life."

—Unknown

Disorganization and chaos breed stress, which breeds sickness and disease. It also wastes your most precious asset, time. I know people who don't keep passwords in one secure place, so everytime they need one it's a frantic search. WHY? Makes ZERO sense! Set up your environment—especially where you work on and in your business—for success. Create peace and harmony visually, auditorily and even in the scents you allow.

With so many of us working from home, I think I have to bring this up... Don't work from your bed! The psychology of that is beyond crazy! Your bed is the place for relaxation, sleep and intimacy with your spouse. It's the opposite energy of what you need in your business. If you can help

"If you want to fly, give up everything that weighs you down."

—Buddha

it, don't even have your desk in your bedroom. Maintain clean and clear boundaries between the energetic fields within your house. Research EMF blocking devices and natural solutions and find what works for you...meaning you will use it consistently.

Speaking of those energetic fields, pay attention to what you are allowing to enter your ears, eyes and mind with music and entertainment. And the social programming they call "news". All of that carries and actually is frequency. Even if you think you're not paying attention with your conscious mind, your subconscious mind doesn't have the filters of reason and analytical skills. It accepts what it perceives as truth. Song lyrics, violence, anti-family and gender confusion agendas labeled "tolerance" and other such nonsense—it's all getting into you if you allow those frequencies.

Your destiny and the destiny of your business is worth paying attention to and nurturing by keeping your energy free and clear and high. You are designed to soar! You are limitless and magnificent and don't need whatever the advertising mind controllers say you can't live without. You run your own race and go after your own God-given dreams—not what culture or your family or anyone else says you have to go after.

Stepping off my soapbox. Thank you for listening.

Mindset and Beliefs

The NUMBER ONE determinant of success is mindset. What you believe about a thing, how you categorize it, or frame it up in context will determine how you respond or react to it. Your thoughts and feelings, which influence each other, drive your behaviors and either attract or repel things, people, and circumstances into your experience.

The awesome thing is...we get to choose our thoughts!

Obviously there are whole academies focused on how mindset—the power of our subconscious and super-conscious—affect our world, so that whole discussion is beyond the scope of this book. I addressed mindset as the first "*Planning to Profit*" in my previous book because some people go into business with an "I don't want to make money" mindset. (Sometimes sugar-coated like, "I only want to help people".) If you're not planning to profit...why even start a business?!

I'm just saying it's a thing, a BIG thing. I'm here to help if you or your ancestral line has deep-seated money mindset issues that are blocking your success. Just book a Liebust session at SpiritCenteredBusiness.com/healing to get started.

Break Through Barriers and Break Off Limits

The purity of our thoughts and motivations has a huge impact on our effectiveness in co-creating our destiny. There is science that backs this up, and you can read about experiments in books such as Lynne Taggert's *The Intention Experiment*. Here's a tangible example that comes to mind: You hear about clouds of gold dust appearing when people are praising and worshiping the Lord...but as soon as they turn it into a parlor trick it goes away. Another example is Peter taking his singular focus off Jesus and starting to sink. (see Matt 14:22-33) Point being, the more clear and focused you can keep your mind and energy (thoughts and feelings), and the more aligned you are with our Source's plan for your life, the quicker and easier it will unfold around you.

Unfortunately, unknown and unseen subconscious or unconscious "slime" can clog up or totally block our ability to operate in the kind of purity of focus I'm talking about. We touched on this here and there, and this is not the place for a deep dive, but I want to address it in this chapter because the impact you have on this earth depends on your inner world, and what's going on there.

We unwittingly make inner vows based on lies that then inform our thoughts, feelings and behaviors. Trauma of any kind, from a stubbed toe to a betrayal to abuse or combat, gets stored in our soul and body tissues. Even generational slime that happened centuries ago can be carried in the DNA of our bodies and in the spirit realm. Even though you didn't make the agreement, the legal paperwork of it still stands in the heavenly courts, giving the enemy the right to harass you and keep you from your destiny.

Henrich, a world-changing Fusion* client in Australia, was having issue after issue in his beverage manufacturing business. A major piece of equipment wasn't working and expert after expert suggested solutions that didn't fix it. Thousands of dollars were going into a black hole. On top of that sales were sluggish and deals fell through. Henrich was exhausted, overwhelmed, and disillusioned with the promise that God was with him in this business. He is very powerful in the spirit realm—to the point of people being healed with one word. So of course the evil one wants to distract him and shut him down. In a session we discovered a spiritual portal the enemy had set up in his home. Holy

Spirit stopped us from destroying it, and instead we cleansed it and it became a trade route. Three days later he received funding for a permanent solution to the failing equipment.

In another session he was beating himself up with the lie that he wasn't where he thought he would be in life, and feeling like a hypocrite because he was so powerful in healing others, but couldn't heal his wife. We divorced the "Perfect Henrich" illusion that was set up as a false identity. We also discovered that his ancestors twenty-one generations ago had plugged into a power source that demanded "toil" as the payment. We broke that covenant and asked Jesus what the result of that was. He heard, "The harvest will now make it all the way to the barns, and you will have full storehouses." Great! ...but I asked Jesus what that looked like in Henrich's real world. "Beverage customers coming in with orders." Awesome. Now he had something to focus on and look for. About a half hour after we got off that zoom I got a Whatsapp from him:

"Just so u know...8 mins after we finished... and after we defined what full storehouses meant...got confirmation of an order for a big customer. Essentially doubled for December. 8 mins."

YAY GOD!!! And just for context...his beverage customers are companies like Pepsi-co. We're not talking about a couple thousand dollars here.

*Fusion coaching is spiritual business coaching,
plus inner healing and heavenly courtroom work with
the help of a trained seer. Learn more:
SpiritCenteredBusiness.com/fusion*

Lies We Build Belief Systems On

Contracts and agreements in the spirit realm are real. They have real world consequences.

The most common agreements we unwittingly come into are Fear, Rejection and Unworthiness. The words we use reveal what agreements we've made in our inner world. Those play out in so many lies:

- I'm not ___ enough.
- I don't deserve _____.
- My family has always been this way, so that's my fate too.
- What will people think/say?
- They rejected my offer therefore they don't like me and I'm not good enough.
- I can't take it.
- What if I fail?
- I can't trust anyone.
- I'm too tired to _____.
- That happens for other people, but not for me.
- It's always going to be this way.
- There's no way out.
- I can't afford to _____.
- I can't hear God.
- ...and any number of other limiting beliefs.

[I renounce and cancel those lies I just read. I clear the negative energy they created.]

Think about the off-hand way we use language to come into agreement with things:

- I'm catching a cold.
- My (sickness or disease or ailment)...taking ownership of it.
- I'm such an idiot.
- I'm sick and tired of _____.
- I'm clumsy.
- BIGGIE: I'm sorry. Think about what that really means. "I apologize", or "I sympathize", or "I feel your pain" is more accurate.

[I renounce and cancel those lies I just read. I clear the negative energy they created.] I wouldn't want you to unwittingly come into agreement just by reading them!

"For out of the abundance of the heart the mouth speaks. A good man out of the good treasure of his heart brings forth good things, and an evil man out of the evil treasure brings forth evil things. But I say to you that for every idle word men may speak, they will give account of it in the day of judgment. For by your words you will be justified, and by your words you will be condemned."

—Mat 34b-37 (NKJV)

If any of the statements above triggered you, or triggered other lies, be sure to break those agreements. Find out what and where the root is so you can pull out all the tendrils associated with it and get healing. As always, I'm here to help. SpiritCenteredBusiness.com/healing

Lies and slime such as false accusations or word curses can also be woven into your business, effectively putting the kibosh on momentum and growth, either on the whole, or in a particular area. But, never fear, those can be cleaned up and broken off too.

Susan from Canada attended a conference where I was speaking, and contacted me for a session. When we met she told me how desperate her financial situation was, and yet she was "terrified" of getting a job because of the traumatic abuse she had suffered in her last one. I stopped her from repeating and elaborating on the story. (That only drives it deeper into your psyche and physiology.) Instead, we prayed and asked Jesus what He wanted to help her with in the session. He said she didn't trust that He loved her all the time. We found roots of this in her bloodline on both Mom and Dad's side, as well as in her own life. She repented and broke agreements with all the lies and slime the enemy had embedded, received forgiveness and replaced those lies with truth. At the end of our session I had her write out all of the truth as declarations so she could reprogram her mind according to God's word rather than the negative experiences.

She texted me about a half hour later:

"I have a WOW to share!

When we finished, I wrote down the declarations
I was receiving. As soon as I finished I picked up the phone
to check something and it started to ring. It was an offer
to do some work for the rest of the summer that is good pay
with flexibility. I know it's the beginning of "the best"
yet to come!!

WOOT-*woot! He is so* AWESOME!!"

Yes, He is!

Symptoms of Hidden Lies or Agreements in Your Business

- Recurring patterns that aren't getting resolved
- Problems for which solutions aren't working
- Low morale or infighting and sabotage
- Marketing isn't attracting leads
- Low sales conversion rates
- Unexpected expenses or losses
- Can't seem to meet/hire the right people
- Deals falling through
- Equipment or technology breaking or failing
- Can't get traction or momentum
- Lack of motivation or excitement for your work

Of course there may be other reasons for these issues, but once you've ruled out best practices, systems and processes...look for the spiritual root. Or just go there directly and follow Heaven's lead on how to clean up the 3D world stuff. (My choice! ☺)

Legacy

Taking responsibility for the lives your business touches (INTENT critical)

We are called Kings and Priests in the Bible. Both Kings and Priests are responsible for taking care of the people they serve, or their citizens. As king of your business, you have responsibility for the lives your business touches. Especially employees. Their families depend on the income you provide. That one is obvious, but there are many lives you touch that aren't so obvious.

Regardless if you connect on a daily basis, or only meet once, remember that you represent your business in every interaction. And people are watching and judging. When you're building a Kingdom business, you also represent the King.

Shifting Culture

Ultimately, the solution you bring to the world through your business changes lives. You make people's lives easier, more organized, more beautiful, more efficient. You uplevel or enhance their experience of life and their expression as a human. The outflow/giving of your finances also has the opportunity to transform culture and build God's Kingdom. This impact matters. Take it seriously.

1. Sinclair, David. "What and When to Eat for Longevity | Lifespan with Dr. David Sinclair #2." YouTube, uploaded by David Sinclair, Jan 12, 2022, https://youtu.be/wD8reCw3Kls.
2. Huberman Lab Podcast:
   https://www.youtube.com/@hubermanlab

CHAPTER 7

ABOUT PRAYERS AND DECLARATIONS

So...What's the Difference?

Prayers are framed up in making your requests known, repentance, breaking agreement with blocks and hindrances, and expressing gratitude and trust. They can be as simple as, "God, Help me," or as specific as identifying the exact legal right the enemy has to use against you and breaking that agreement. For the purposes of this work, we will direct prayers to the Godhead.

Declarations are decrees made from your kingly authority in Christ (if you're in Christ as a Son), and we will direct them to ourselves and to the universe as statements of how we are to be in alignment with who our Creator made us to be, and the destiny He gave us. These come from a co-creative, becoming stance. Simply put, a declaration is a truth that exists in the spirit realm, and may or may not exist yet in the natural realm.

"Prayer is not only worship;
it is also an invisible emanation of
man's worshiping spirit—the most
powerful form of energy that one
can generate."

—Dr. Alexis Carrel

Affirmations are statements that affirm an established truth that we often need to remind ourselves of, especially in those moments when we're not acting as the magnificent being we were designed to be.

Esther's Example

In the biblical book of Esther we see the difference and the need for both prayers and declarations. In chapter four Queen Esther and her maids prayed and fasted for three days, repenting, worshiping, asking for and receiving strategies to stand against the evil of Haman. The story unfolds, the foe is vanquished, and Queen Esther and Mordecai have victory. But just because the enemy was defeated doesn't mean all the hell he caused was gone. The curse still had to be reversed. In chapter eight Esther and Mordecai had to write out and declare the new vision of the future they desired to see. It was scribed, announced and sealed with the king's signet ring.

Introduction to Declarations

When you accept Yeshua into your spirit, surrendering your plan for His plan, and allowing Him to take the reins, you have the added authority of a Son of God. If you haven't made this commitment yet, don't worry. These declarations will still have a measure of power in the spirit realm because they operate spiritual principles that work no matter who you are. It's like gravity; you can not understand it, you can deny it, and you can try to work against it, but it still always works.

The most important, or obvious, declaration, as they relate to your business destiny, is your foundation document, the Declaration of Trade, which includes the Deed of Commerce and Trade. (This is for believers who have accepted Christ as their Savior and Lord because it states He is the owner and CEO of your business, which equates to the Lord of your life—which isn't true unless you surrender to Him. See the Bonus Prayers section for that prayer.)

The Declaration of Trade is more than just a legal establishing document. When you work with Heaven and really think about what your business is going be and do, and the impact it will have, those declarations carry weight. They inform your business model, your brand identity, your marketing, your culture, your positioning, your operations, and even your family, home and health.

When Tim first came to me his business was in chaos. Everyone was frustrated with each other, projects were running into snag after snag and taking longer than they should. Customers were upset and nerves were frazzled. After we broke off the false accusations and closed the open access points from the past, it was time to declare a new future. Some issues cleared up immediately, and once he created his Declaration of Trade all chaos stopped. Technical tangles literally sorted themselves out. The team was able to see a clear path forward and got back to operating in harmony...just as he declared they would in his Dec of Trade.

Leo had done his Dec of Trade, but wasn't stewarding it well. He hadn't even read it lately, much less sat with it and meditated over it with Yahweh. His businesses had reverted back to their disorganized, indifferent and back-biting state from before he came to work with me. In one of our coaching sessions he realized he needed to continue making the declarations and pay attention to where the "little foxes" came in. He closed those doors and called his businesses back to the "on earth as it is in heaven" state he had declared. The next week he reported that doors of opportunity opened up and he was able to get a meeting with a high level person in the Mexican government. A team member who would normally be put off by making the trip to Mexico City eagerly came with him, and the meeting went very smoothly. Over the next few weeks every time we met Leo had another testimony of healing, break-through, or momentum gained. One session he even reported that clients in his insurance business were seeking him out to pay him—totally opposite of the usual chasing them to be paid. Yay God!!!

Setting Your Intention and Declaring it Aloud

You've already written the vision, bringing it from the spirit realm into the natural in 2D form. Now you need to release it with your voice. First, the words you speak are influencing YOU. They help you make the shift into total belief and knowing they are true even if they haven't manifested in your physical experience yet. Secondly, your voice sends out a vibrational frequency that carries the intent you place behind the words you say. That's why it's important to focus on the appropriate positive intent, and charge them up with as much emotion as possible.

Bringing Your Future Into Your Now

We, as humans, are the only life form created on Earth that can consciously choose to harmonize the frequency of our brain and heart so they become a single focused system.[1]

We can literally harness the power of our body to generate a frequency pattern that can travel through dimensions and across time.

Science shows us that thoughts produce an electrical charge and feelings produce a magnetic charge. So how you think, and how you feel produces an electromagnetic signature that influences everything in your life.[2]

Performing over 600 experiments, researcher René Peoc'h showed that baby chicks who thought of a small robot as their mother could influence its behavior. When left on its own, the robot randomly moved around the room. [See Figure A] When chicks placed in a cage at one end of the room "called" to their "mother", the robot spent considerably more time in that area, and didn't even travel to the other end of the room. [See Figure B] You can see the re-created experiment in the YouTube video[3] noted below. See also the supporthealth.com[4] article about this experiment referenced at the end of the chapter. It's quite remarkable! By the power of their little minds, the chicks influenced the behavior of an object.

My two take-aways are:
1. The chicks held an affection for the robot and desired to be near it, and
2. They consistently voiced their desire, which called it near. Emotionally charged words.

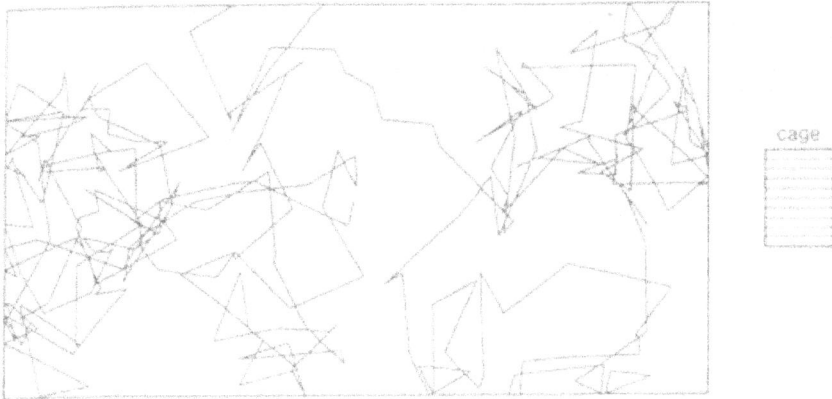

Figure A

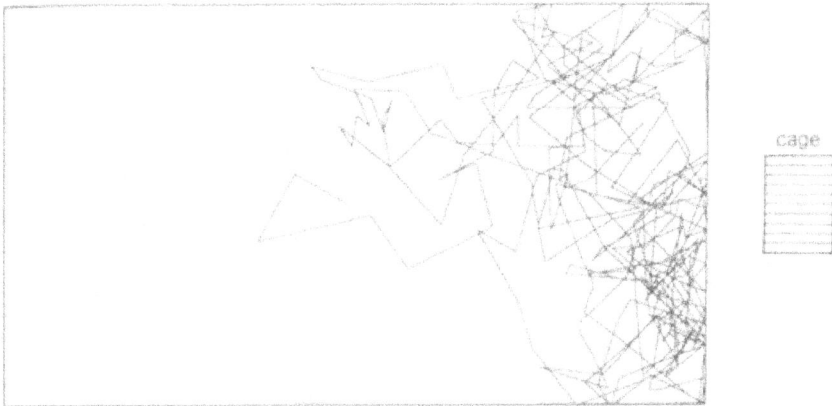

Figure B

Your world is created by your words. The universe and your subconscious are listening, and they are very literal. If you say, "I want a new convertible." The universe is designed to give you exactly that...the want (which means LACK) of a new convertible. You will have and hold this desire for as long as you say those words to yourself. Instead, frame your thoughts and affirmations specifically, in the present tense, preferably using "I am", and add as much sensory language as you can. That will help you bring your body (3D) into the equation with emotions to fuel your words.

Like this, "I am thrilled with the way my new smoky blue Camero ZL1 convertible handles as I cruise with the top down along the Pacific Coast Highway. I love the leather interior with wood trim, and the mag wheels look SO hot. I feel sexy, powerful and free!" (What can I say...I'm a car girl and a speed junky.)

Did you see it with me? Smell the new leather? Feel the wind in your hair and the sun on your face?

When you can FEEL the gratitude and joy of experiencing the object of your desire— that is the special sauce!

Once you work WITH the laws of the universe, intentionally aligning your vibration to that which you desire is easy. Speaking affirmations out loud is important, and managing our thoughts is even more critical. Here's why: We speak an average of 10-20 thousand words each day, but we think 70,000 thoughts a day. Take every thought captive. Hold onto and repeat the truths, and banish the lies.

When we speak our declarations out loud, it activates our thoughts, emotions and auditory function—and if we look into our eyes in a mirror while we say them, it also activates our visual function. Really rev up the effectiveness by including physical movement!

Therefore it's imperative that you BELIEVE your affirmations, that you actually THINK they will work and are true for you in the quantum realm—which is the future you in the 3D realm.

Here's a ramp up to belief, if you need one. Begin your declaration statements with 1, then 2, then 3 progressively. Don't move from 1 until you feel in your body that it is true for you.

1. I choose..., or I desire to...
2. I am willing to...
3. I am ready to...

When each one feels true for you in your body, move to the next until you are ready to fully embrace and declare, "I am..."

But wait...there's one more REALLY important step. Check in with Father to see if what you are thinking about declaring is what He wants for you right now. Is it on your destiny scroll, and is this the right timing? I don't know about you, but I'm really DONE trying to do my business (and life) the way *I* think is best. Not only have I made some big messes, but when it's all about me, I have to do it in my own strength—AND pay for it! Ugh. I'd rather do it the way the Creator of the universe already planned, resourced, and prepared the way for me to do it. It's also pretty important to be in the right timing. So ask if the time is now while you're asking if the WHAT is correct. Funny— but Father knows your WHY too. So be sure your motives and heart position are in alignment as well.

Okay, moving on to the HOW.

Visualize

In case you jumped to this bit, here's a brief overview from the *Envision Your Ideal Destiny* part above. Visualization is one of the most powerful exercises you can do to transform your life. When you visualize, you are materializing in the spirit realm an ideal future to bring into the physical realm. You can create a dramatization of the life you want to live. When you visualize, ask Holy Spirit to reveal the destiny of your business. Watch it play out in your imagination. You can see it in the present, as detailed and crisp as a movie. This will remind you of how close your destiny is. This creates specific thoughts and feelings that will lead you to manifesting it in the physical realm.

Allow and Receive

The final step is to allow your business destiny to manifest into reality, receiving it, and embracing it—even though it may not look like what you thought it would. This seems relatively straightforward, but in fact, many people struggle to believe they are worthy to receive gifts, success, influence, and so on. To accomplish this step, you must make the choice to move toward the life you've envisioned.

You may benefit from an inner healing Liebusting session, which breaks off limiting beliefs that hold you back and shifts your mindset to the truth. We also use this process to shift and clear energy. Negative emotions are negative energy. When they aren't processed, they get stored in the body, so even though we're working on other things, my clients often have physical healing as well. To book a session visit: www.SpiritCenteredBusiness.com/healing.

Each time you use these declarations, I invite you to do so from a higher perspective. Operating these principles as a Son of God—and ladies you are also "Sons" in position and authority when you accept Yeshua. That means you are at rest, seated on your throne in heaven, and making decrees and declarations as a royal king. If you are not yet a son of God, you may ask Yeshua's permission for a visitor's pass to the throne room, or wherever He may guide you. I would advise against breaking and entering...it won't go well, so just leave it alone. (See John 10:1) You are totally loved and fully accepted just as you are, so there's no need to prove yourself to God, or sneak around like an interloper. Just ask for permission, and listen for the go-ahead. Possibly there are things God wants you to do before you get the go-ahead. We all need to respect Father's throne room. Just like some homes have a no shoes policy, so you don't go traipsing in without removing them at the door. There's no condemnation, just do whatever He would have you do, and proceed.

Close your physical eyes, and open your spiritual ones. It may take a minute for the blackness of the back of your eyelids to fade back, but keep looking. You may just sense something, hear a sound or a voice, or just know it without knowing how. Trust your gut, and go with your first instinct. It may take practice, but you don't have to wait to see/sense. In the spirit realm, operating by faith, meaning in the certainty and expectancy that what you are doing is real and meaningful, is just as important as having a spiritual experience you can describe.

Visualize yourself in God's throne room, either seated on your throne or standing, addressing the court. Angels, elders, witnesses, the seven spirits of God, and other spiritual beings will most likely be there. If you get a different scene, like a mountaintop, or a conference room, just go with it. The right personnel will be there if you invite them.

Now, the laws of quantum physics show you can be in multiple places at once. Let's go for just three. Your body will most likely remain wherever you left it. LOL. (Although I have met people who took their bodies with them—let's not get distracted.) Your spirit/soul will be in the place of declaration as we just discussed. Your spirit and soul can also be forward in your timeline to experience that outcome of your declaration, which allows you to get into the best emotional state to make a powerful proclamation. I know...I can't get my mind around it either, but practice has shown me that it works regardless of my understanding of the mechanics of it.

In a strong, authoritative voice declare out loud whatever statement or statements in the next section you choose. You may also choose to anchor the statement into your physical body with a gesture, such as a fist pump, reserved only for peak emotional state moments. This will help you get back to that state when you need to.

1. Braden, Gregg. "How You Can Create An Amazing Reality For Yourself | Gregg Braden." YouTube, uploaded by Gregg Braden Official, March 3, 2020, https://youtu.be/bb8rZl8sKSU.
2. Dispenza, Joe. "How To Reprogram Your Subconscious Mind To Manifest Your Dream Future! | Joe Dispenza." YouTube, uploaded by Lewis Howes, Oct. 7, 2022, https://youtu.be/c7nxcCSjjRM.
3. Peoc'h, Rene. "LA MENTE ACTÚA SOBRE LA MATERIA." YouTube, uploaded by Mariano Casaca, Apr 10, 2013, https://youtu.be/mR9Ew-MW43s.
4. https://www.supporthealth.com.au/rene-peoch-chickens-telekinesis/

SECTION TWO

Prayers and Declarations
to Steward and Stand

CHAPTER 8

PRAYERS AND DECLARATIONS TO STEWARD AND STAND

I separated prayers and declarations, but in real life, they get blended together, and it's no big deal. However, when you're stewarding and standing on God's promises and co-creating with him, it's best to stick with the declaration format, as described in the previous chapter. That's why many of the following sections will only have declarations, and no prayers. Declarations are more authoritative and bring your body and all of creation around you into alignment with the "it-is-finished" frequency that pulls it out of the spirit realm into the physical realm.

Of course, you will be able to quickly and easily turn a prayer into a declaration, or visa versa once you understand the difference. Quick review: You want a prayer when you need to repent of something or are asking for something. You want a declaration when you, with "clean hands" (already asked for forgiveness and changed your behavior) and a "pure heart" (motives in alignment with God's will) need to decree a thing shall be.

Because the efficacy of prayers and declarations does not depend on the number of words you use, you'll find most of these are quite short and to the point. Totally doable! I invite you to "selah", or pause and think after speaking out each one. (And after the first read through, you won't be doing more than one or two at a time.) Check in with your spirit and Holy Spirit. Ask what changed because I prayed or declared that? Please show me. Also pay attention to your body. See if anything feels lighter or more free. Note any changes and pay attention to this area of business. Watch for clues of the destiny you declared manifesting!

If anything shifted, we would love to hear about it! Please share your testimony on SpiritCenteredBusiness.com/ businessdestinybook, or wherever you find us on social media.

Just one more confession...I only know my field, and perhaps a touch of the fields of my clients. So please forgive me if topics specific to your industry are not included here. Hopefully you will be able to take the gist of these prayers and declarations, meditate with Holy Spirit, and create some of your own, unique to your situation. In fact, I declare that you will!

You may come across unfamiliar language or concepts as you read and activate these prayers and declarations. Many Biblical truths are not taught in churches, so don't feel left out. Because teaching them is outside the scope of this book, I opted to build a library of brief teachings called *Kingdom Concepts* on our website instead. Visit SpiritCenteredBusiness.com/businessdestinybook to find them.

Business Destiny

Trust in the Process, and Dedicate to God

Prayer:

Creator, I thank you for my divine design and plan for my life. I honor you as my Source, my Protector and my Provider. Thank you for designing me with an entrepreneurial spirit and giving me the authority and mandate to transform lives through my business. Please forgive me for those times when I've operated outside your best plan and tried to do things in my own power. I lay down my plan for yours, and accept the destiny you've designed for me and for my business. I trust that your plan is much better, will align my skills, talents and energy better, and will touch more people in a more profound way. Let my business be a light to the world, a beacon of hope, and a solution to the problems of those people you have already determined I will serve. Thank you for this amazing destiny! I receive it with open arms and an open heart to be your hands and feet on the earth and to impact my industry with your love.

Declaration:

I declare that God Most High has an amazing plan for my business, and that I fully trust Him and surrender to the process of pulling it down from heaven and walking it out on the earth. I declare that I am bold and courageous and make no agreement with fear. Though rejection, set-backs, or discouragement may come, I draw a line in the sand and declare them powerless to keep me from my mission. I now dedicate (rededicate) my business to God as an integral facet of the personal destiny He gave me. Let my mark upon this earth stand as a testament to the goodness and glory of God and His plan for me and for my business.

Clarity of Vision and Holy Spirit Leading

(Speak out only the documents you have or need and skip the rest. Feel free to add any as well. The point is to make what you see in the spirit realm manifest in the natural.)

Declaration:

I declare that I have received the documents of establishment of my business in the spirit realm. I further declare that I see these documents clearly, with the details that I need to know today readable and understandable. I now have in my possession a full and complete set, including a Declaration of Trade and Deed of Commerce and Trade, a strategic business plan, resource allocation list, outflow plan, operating manual or bylaws, required permits, and any other legal documents required to fulfill my mandate. I declare these documents are properly filed in heaven and on earth*, and the Certificate of Formation and Establishment has been received and is on display in both realms. I declare that Father, Jesus, Holy Spirit, people in white linen, and angels appointed to my business destiny, as well as the Seven Spirits of God, and any other assigned beings are guiding me to full manifestation of my mandate here on earth. I declare that no weapon or evil scheme designed to keep this destiny from unfolding will see success.

Leave "on earth" out if you have not yet created these documents in the natural.

Increased Impact and Seeding the Mandate

Declaration:

I declare my business shall have the maximum influence, results and impact allotted by its God-given destiny. No efforts of the enemy to throttle down or bleed off the transformation and problem-solving my business brings to the marketplace shall be successful. I hereby seed my mandate into the territory allocated to my business, geographical, demographical, dimensional and industry-specific. I claim the territory in the airways and across the internet that has been preordained for my business to have. I release angels and spiritual beings to help nurture and grow these good seeds I cover with gold and sow in fertile ground. I call forth 100% of the multiplied harvest of all physical and spiritual fruit predestined for my business to have. I receive it into my treasury rooms and storehouses, payment portals, bank accounts, and even into my hand. In the bountiful name of Yeshua.

Self as Business Owner

"The only person you are destined to become is the person you decide to be."

—Ralph Waldo Emerson

Mindsets: Capable, Value/Worth, Discipline

Combo Prayer and Declaration:

Let it be established across all heavenly and earthly dimensions and realms that I am King and Priest over this enterprise, and all of it, including myself and any and all beings involved are under Yahweh's Kingship. I hereby declare that I am fully equipped and capable of executing the tasks required to establish and operate this business, including having clarity, focus and discipline. I break any and all alignment or agreement with unworthiness, self-doubt, fear, _____, or any other sabotaging belief. I break the power any of these have had over my life or business. Please forgive me for allowing these access through my agreement with them. I declare total confidence in my Spirit-led abilities and complete trust in Jehovah Jireh as my provider. I furthermore declare that I am valued and valuable regardless of, and separate from the success of my business. I agree to operate this business as a faithful, disciplined and dedicated steward, worthy of Father's, "Well done."

Expanded Consciousness and Capacity

Declaration:

I declare I have the infinite mind of Christ, and that all my skills, abilities, talents and faculties, being established under the authority and ownership of Father God, are abundantly blessed, functioning at peak performance and capacity, and are infinitely resilient and expandable to execute any and all tasks related to the mandate and destiny of my business. I declare that I am emotionally intelligent, and easily rise above situations that attempt to trigger discord in my soul. I am able to remain steady, calm and sharp in stressful situations. I further declare that as I build my business, I simultaneously build the necessary structures inside myself required to carry the influence and responsibility of my business. I release and dissolve any structures of thought or belief systems based on lies or false testimony. I request and agree to receive the counsel given to me by Heaven in this regard.

Hint: That counsel may come through humans. Pay attention if someone calls out or triggers your emotional instability or your use of limiting language.

Health, Family/Life Balance and Blessing Declaration:

I declare that in the ebb and flow of activity in my business, the rest of my life is also attended to and blessed. I declare that I have sufficient time to nourish my family relationships, my health and physical well-being, my passions outside of business, and my community. Though aspects of my life take a higher or lower precedence in their seasons, I declare here and now that I will neither neglect nor abandon my health, my family, nor any other important relationships or responsibilities because of my business. I honor and bless the people in my life; my life is enhanced because of them. I also bless my body as a magnificent vessel of God's presence, and the vehicle by which I do His work here on earth.

Clients, Customers and Audience

More of Them

Declaration:

Let it be known across heavenly realms and on earth that my ideal clients are now coming to me. People who have the need that my unique business solves easily and quickly for them are headed my way. I declare an increase of clients and customers from known and unknown sources and places. I commission the angels on assignment to turn their attention toward me and bring them in.

I further declare that the online territory I have claimed and staked across social media platforms and anywhere my digital footprint exists is now magnetized by Heaven's power. I infuse every piece of my content, and every favorable mention of me, my business, or my products or services with frequency that makes people feel loved and safe. I declare my audience on all platforms where I can be found is growing, engaged, and benefitted by what I bring to the table. Let it be so in the mighty name of Jesus.

Blessing Them

Prayer: (This is mine. You may insert your mandate and mission here.)

Thank you, Lord, that I have the privilege and honor to serve these amazing people you have set aside for me. I am humbled that you would trust me with the responsibility of unblocking, unlocking, and setting them free! Thank you for giving me unique strategies to recover and restore their lost, stolen, traded away, abandoned or deteriorated influence. I trust you to give me the proper words at the proper time to activate them and help them manifest and steward their destinies. In the infinite name of Jesus I pray, Amen.

Declaration:

I hereby gather all former, present and future clients into my business realm and release blessings over them. I declare them blessed financially, physically, relationally and spiritually. I declare their families and relationships filled with peace, joy and love. I release bonds of abundance, harmony, health and well-being over them right now, directly from the heart of Yahweh. Let it be known that my clients, customers and audience receive the full measure of healing, breakthrough, clarity and revelation our Father in heaven intends for them. I seal these blessings across all timelines, ages, realms and dimensions in the powerful name of Jesus the Christ.

Attracting the Right Ones

Declaration:

I declare that I have diligently done my market research to define the demographics and psychographics of my ideal clients. I fully understand their pain and problems, and can speak in the language of their thoughts, feelings and dreams. This draws them to me like a magnet.

Father, as CEO of my business, and the Creator of my destiny, you have already predetermined the people I am to touch through my business. Therefore I hereby declare that none of them will fall to the wayside. The ones you have set aside for me will see my marketing and avail themselves of the solutions I offer. I further declare that no tire kickers or time wasters who are not the set aside ones you have for me will distract me or take me off my purpose.

Finances and Resources

Heavenly Abundance

Declaration:

Jehovah Jireh, my Provider, my Source of all good things, I trust you. I declare that you have given me the power to create wealth and set me as your trusted steward over this business to make it prosper. I hereby establish my business as a portal for you to flow finances and financial favor into so I may flow them out to build your kingdom. Let it be known in heaven and on earth that this assignment you have given me has been fully funded. I lack nothing expedient to its full execution.

I declare the treasure rooms and storehouses of heaven are opened to me and my associates. I commission angels of finance to bring to my business all that has been appointed to me. I establish trade routes between all applicable sources of finance and wealth and my treasury in heaven, through dimensional portals to my earthly bank accounts and even to my hands. Sentry angels, I commission you to guard and protect these routes and access points so that nothing may be stolen, lost, abandoned or deteriorated, and nothing that is not of God may come through. I erect a shield over the entire operation so it may be completely camouflaged to the agents of darkness, and I set the dials to stealth mode.

I hereby set the hours of operation of these routes, the guardians, and the caravans that traverse them as 24/7/365 in time and out of time and across all timelines and dimensions. I declare an acceleration of time so that as I sow I reap, even to the degree that reaping overtakes sowing. So it shall be on earth as it is in heaven in the mighty, abundant name of Yeshua Hamashiach.

Proper Stewardship and Nurturing

Prayer:

Jehovah, please forgive me for not stewarding my gifts and talents, or the business you gave me to the best of my ability. I break agreement with laziness, just sliding by, and operating on a default of passivity. I lay these and all of the associated habits and thought patterns at your feet, Yeshua. I ask you to break the cycle of mediocrity and settling for less than excellence in my work. Forgive me for not nurturing my business, forgetting that it's actually yours. I ask for your grace and mercy in the places where I've neglected to put the energy, time and thought into my business. Please forgive me for not honing my skills and seeking after wisdom and understanding to continue to develop my craft and my business savvy. I need a fresh start, and I need your guidance and guardrails to help me not slip back into complacency. I receive my forgiveness, and I rededicate my skills and energy to serving well those you have predestined for me to serve. Please let me hear your "Well done, good and faithful steward." In the mighty name of Yeshua I pray. Amen.

Declaration:

I decree and declare that I am a faithful steward. I am knowledgeable and wise in all my financial dealings. As I sow generously into fertile soil and nourish and incubate those seeds in intentional, faith-filled prayer, You will grow them, Lord. I speak life and blessing to the work of my hands, and the decisions I have made with Heaven's counsel. I flow the river of life through my business, my bank accounts, my investments, my strategic relationships, and anything else under my stewardship. Let that living water restore, revitalize, strengthen and grow everything it touches.

I declare that fear and doubt related to finances are bound in chains and kept far from me and from my thoughts. Let me think, speak and act only according to your Love and Truth.

Protection, Including Legal and Insurance

Prayer:

Divine Protector, thank you for the grace you've given me to this point in my business. Thank you for supernaturally protecting me, my family and associates, and everything under my stewardship. Please forgive me for missing anything in the natural that I should have put in place for protection, whether by ignorance, neglect or poor choices. I ask for divine covering that would keep financial hardships, legal issues, sickness, disease, accidents and time wasting annoyances far from me, my family and associates, and anything related to my business.

Where there is already damage done I repent for my part in it, and ask for a reversal and divine clean up as if it never happened. Please guide me to trustworthy help and solutions that are honoring and in alignment with your Kingdom principles and plan for my life and business. In the mighty name of Jesus I pray, amen.

Creativity and Solutions

Plenty, Endless Source, and Ease of Flow

Prayer:

Creator of the universe, thank you for creating me in your image. Thank you for shaping my mind and designing my abilities and giftings specifically for the destiny you gave me. Thank you for trusting me with stewarding the destiny of my business. I am humbled and grateful. You see the challenges I'm facing right now, and know the exact solutions my clients and customers need. I ask for your creativity in every area of my business: branding, marketing and graphic design, copy of all kinds, products that express my uniqueness and distinction in the marketplace. I ask for creative ways to nurture relationships and create win-win solutions and honorable communication.

Source of all, I thank you that your well of creativity never runs dry, and that my team and I are allowed to freely tap into it. I trust you for fresh ideas that flow easily each and every time we need them. I cover the channel of creativity between you and me with heavenly gold. I bless my imagination and invite you to download innovations, strategy and divine brilliance at any time, whether I am asleep or awake. Bring to my remembrance any previously downloaded ideas in the moment I need them.

I bind any entities or powers that would try to come against my creativity, or that of my team, or anyone associated with my business. Confusion, stuckness, mediocrity, frustration, blankness, overwhelm, fatigue and laziness are not allowed to interfere with my creativity in any way. I set my expectancy on receiving supernatural solutions in the moment I need them. Please don't let anything you're doing on my behalf escape my notice. I expect miracles today. In Yeshua's infinite name, amen.

Declaration:

I declare the portals and channels of creativity are open, cleansed and flowing to me now. I sanctify my imagination and declare it holy. By faith I step into the realm of infinite possibilities and boundless creativity. I break any agreements I've made, or that were spoken over me that would hinder the limitless flow of creativity toward me and my business associates. I now choose to receive innovative ideas, unique expressions of my thoughts, dreams and desires, and words and images that attract, inspire and add value to all who see them. By your grace, Lord, let it be so.

Unique and Distinctive

Declaration:

Let it be established that as I am created uniquely, my business and the solution I bring to the marketplace is unique. I declare that my branding, my copy, and my marketing speak to this distinction in a way that is exclusively mine. I decree and declare there shall be no plagiarism, counterfeits or knock-offs of my intellectual property, my products, or anything else defined by my brand. I hereby decree that my brand and business are recognized visually, and by the message and values I bring to the world. I infuse my content, products and services with the distinctive frequency of heaven assigned to my business destiny scroll. I declare it speaks from heaven into the earth realm with a voice print as unique as my own. In the inimitable name of Yeshua, it is so.

Strategies and Tactics to Get Results

Getting heavenly revelation for specific strategies and tactics to achieve the objectives of your business plan requires actually hearing and/or seeing (or perceiving) the Lord. Take your time with this prayer, and keep asking questions. You can even ask what question to ask if you're stuck. Because I'm not a prolific seer, I usually ask if I heard or perceived that correctly. I've also approached this from heaven and made a list of ideas to ask about.

When you turn your attention, or "step into" heaven, be sure to start with an opening prayer like we did when we received the destiny scroll.

Combo Prayer and Declaration:

Father God, I thank you for life and breath, and for loving me enough to create an amazing, hope-filled plan for my future. I ask for an open heaven all around me right now, and I call my spirit forward to connect with my Creator. I ask for a protective barrier around me that expands across time and space so that nothing outside of God's plans and purposes for me will be allowed to interfere or distract me. I declare I'm operating in stealth mode, undetectable by the enemy. Thank you Jesus, for tearing the veil between the dimensions and I step through you as the only door with access to Father's Kingdom. Holy Spirit, please open the eyes and ears of my heart, open my ability to perceive, and don't let me miss anything of what's going on in the spirit realm around me. I trust that I will receive supernatural strategies and the tactics to execute them for my business today, regardless of whether or not I can see or hear. I trust the process by an act of my will, and I declare they will be dropped into my mind as I'm going about my day if I don't overtly receive them now.

Here you will want to state what you are working on and where you are stuck, and listen and watch for the answers to come to you. Keep asking questions. Close with thanksgiving, such as: Thank you, Jesus, my CEO for help in this area. I bless your mighty Name, Amen.

Operations and Technology

Marketing and Sales

Prayer:

Source of All, I ask for your divine strategy for increasing the reach of my marketing efforts to drive business. Let the good seeds I plant by releasing love and the light of your glory to all who see my message be covered with gold and firmly planted in fertile ground. I call for nurturing angels to help grow the brand identity of my products and services. Please show me where and when to make wise investments of my advertising dollars and my time. Let the right people see my message at exactly the moment they are searching for the solution to their problem. Please let my message speak in the language that attracts buyers and compels them to respond.

Father, I ask you to help me and my team to be consistent in putting fresh marketing materials and valuable content and resources out into the world. Let my website, social media pages, and all digital and offline marketing strategies as well as virtual and physical networking gain traction rapidly with supernatural stickiness. I call for angels to turn the heads and open the eyes that need to see me, perk up the ears that need to hear me, and open the minds of those who need to understand that what I offer is the answer to their prayers.

Creator, I ask for wisdom in sales conversations that I would speak the language that resonates with the buyers you already have in place to use my products and services. I ask that you would send angelic help to pave the way for clear, unhindered communication when it comes to expressing my value in the marketplace. I take this opportunity to break off any lies I may have come into agreement with that would cause lack of confidence, hesitation in naming my price, or fear of rejection. I ask for your heavenly perspective to see any sales call from your eternal view, and in the context of the destiny of my business.

I nullify any confusion, obfuscation, or technology hindrances that would render my marketing or sales unsuccessful. I bind and put to sleep any spiritual forces set against my success. By the power of Yeshua I pray. Amen.

Delivery and Distribution

Declaration:

I hereby declare that the products and services I provide are protected along the entire route from concept in the thought realm to manufacturing, to storage, to delivery into my customer's hand. Even the coaching and speaking I do is well thought-out, well articulated, and well-received with no interference or deterioration of the message God would have me share. Every step along the way is guarded by angelic forces assigned to the task, and is blanketed with the oil of ease and flow. Every vehicle and conveyance of any kind, online and offline, is covered in Heaven's protective bubble on every side and above and below. Where my products and services are in proximity to others, I declare that no negative energy or curses of any kind shall touch them. My online content shall reside and be found wherever my intended audience and clients happen to be, unsullied by the adjacent content. My physical products may be manufactured, stored or transported near unwholesome products, but nothing shall taint them. By the intent of my will I infuse blessing and Heaven's frequencies of love, joy, peace and healing into every product and service I offer. I seal these blessings across every timeline, age, realm and dimension in the mighty name of Jesus!

Note: *Yes, this book in your hands has been prayed over, protected and infused! Enjoy!*

Administrative Systems and Processes

Prayer:

Lord, I ask for an ease and a flow of all of the administrative tasks, systems and processes in my business. Please prioritize and sequence my work, and that of my team, so we can focus on what needs to be done and not get distracted or off into the weeds. Show us more efficient ways to do things. Bring cost effective and helpful ideas and tools to our attention. Please let me see where I am wasting time and/or resources, and help me correct the issue. I ask for discernment in knowing which technology tools to implement and when. I deploy angelic help to get things done behind the scenes that create acceleration and ease for my team and me. Thank you for taking care of things before they become problems. I trust that you desire my business to succeed, and for me to stay in my zone of genius as much as I do. Thank you for your help King Jesus! Amen.

Declaration:

As king of my business, I decree and declare that the routine administrative tasks required are supernaturally anointed with the oil of ease. I declare that any repetitive tasks are documented with easy to find and use checklists and templates that can be delegated with minimum training. All of the passwords and login information required for all online interfaces are securely stored and easily accessible only to those who are authorized. All processes are documented and followed efficiently and effectively, and periodically reviewed for updates. I hereby declare that all technological and analog systems are integrated into the workflow of my business and automated to the extent possible at this time. Transactions and interactions are smooth, easy and fruitful, to the delight of my clients and customers, and to the increase of my business. I commission angels to monitor all online systems, and guard against hacking or failure of any kind. I declare all interface points are guarded and protected so that nothing may harm my business or its interests. I seal these declarations across all timelines, ages, realms and dimensions, in the Name above all names, Yeshua Hamashiach.

Relationships, Rapport and Influence

Team, Including Angelic Help

I include some of the characteristics I look for and expect in my team. Feel free to edit or add as you see fit.

Combo:

Jehovah Sabaoth, God of Angel Armies, I thank you that you have made angels ministering spirits to the inheritors of salvation, of which I am as a believer in Christ Jesus. Your Word also says that men and women in white linen are cheering us on to victory as we run our race. Lord, I receive any assistants from heaven that you have appointed to my personal and business destiny scrolls. I honor them and bless them with your Bread of Life and Living Water. I loose angels who operate in all facets of my business: marketing, sales, operations, technology, administration, supply and delivery, logistics, human resources, and every other area. I commission my angels to execute their assignments with excellence as they minister strength and well-being to my body, Wisdom and Understanding to my mind, and orchestrate the unfolding of your plan for my business.

I call forth all of the human team members appointed to my business destiny in their perfect timing. I declare my team is dedicated, loyal, faithful, creative, resourceful, talented, fun, adventurous, forward-thinking, forerunning, heaven-walking, punctual, attentive to detail, community/team oriented, self-starting, ambitious, trustworthy, honest, courteous, witty, clean, organized, effective and efficient. I bless them with health, vitality, and fulfilling relationships outside of working with me. I declare that my business prospers, and I can pay my team well and bless them over and above their salaries. Furthermore, I decree and declare that they shall be blessed in the city, blessed in the country, blessed coming in and blessed going out. Everything they put their hands to shall succeed.

Let a supernaturally protective barrier be hereby established across all timelines, realms and dimensions that guards both my heavenly and my earthly team members and their families. I ask for sentries and warring angels, so that all gateways, bridges and interface points of any kind in any dimension are guarded and protected on all sides, above and below. I declare that no weapon formed against them shall prosper. In the mighty Name of Yeshua I pray, amen.

Connections and Opportunities

Declaration:

Let it be known in heaven and on earth that I have the best angels on assignment to orchestrate divine encounters and mutually beneficial connections. I commission them to work in and out of time to make sure I meet the people I need to meet, see the signs I need to see, and am in the right place at the right time. I declare my team and I have supernatural favor on us in all of our business dealings. People are attracted to us and our marketing, and they bless us in delightful ways. I have rapport with the clients and customers you have preordained for me to serve. They see me, like me, am blessed by me, and repeatedly do business with me because of the bond we share. Opportunities flow to me, and I am easily able to discern which ones are on my destiny scroll and which ones will be distractions. Thank you, Lord, for growing my network of enthusiastic fans who tell others about my work and business so I am able to grow my influence and impact for your Kingdom on the earth. Let it be so in the Awesome Power of Jesus the Christ.

Communication, Negotiation and Money Conversations

Prayer:

Wise Counselor, please guide and direct me in my business dealings with my team, clients, vendors and anyone I communicate with. Guard my mouth that I don't speak out of turn, disparagingly, or falsely. Let my words be clear and precise, flowing articulately in truth and love. Please let my face and body language be aligned with my words. If there are decisions to be made, guide me towards choices that align with your will and honor you. Grant me discernment to recognize opportunities for generosity and compassion, even in the midst of financial challenges. I also lift up the other individuals involved in these conversations. Let your Wisdom touch their hearts as well, leading us all towards understanding and cooperation. May our interactions be marked by mutual respect and a desire to find solutions that benefit all parties involved.

During these conversations, I release your overwhelming peace to calm any anxieties or fears that may arise. Please give me the strength to remain patient and composed, even in the face of challenges or disagreements. Above all, Lord, help me to stand on the Truth that my worth and identity are not defined by material possessions, nor by my performance, but by your Love. Keep my heart focused on your eternal promises, guiding me to seek first your Kingdom and righteousness. I place these money conversations into your hands, trusting that you will guide me in the right direction. In Jesus' name, I pray. Amen.

Conflict Resolution and Boundaries

Prayer for Conflict Resolution:

Lord, I acknowledge that conflicts are a part of human relationships, but I also know that You call us to be peacemakers. Help me to approach this conflict with a spirit of humility, understanding, and a desire for reconciliation. Give me the strength to set aside my own pride and ego, and to listen with an open heart to the concerns of others. I ask Ruach Hakodesh (Holy Spirit) to be present in all interactions related to this conflict. Soften our hearts and grant us the ability to see each other through your eyes. Help us to see past our differences and to recognize the common ground we share as your beloved children. Father, I invite Wisdom to guide my words and actions. Let me speak with grace and truth, always seeking to build bridges rather than walls. Give me the patience to persevere in seeking resolution, even when the path seems difficult. Show me the outcome you desire so I can set my course toward it. In the Name of the King of Peace, Amen.

Declaration for Healthy Boundaries:

I hereby declare to my soul and to the universe that I know I am fearfully and wonderfully made by, and in the image of the Creator. My worth is not determined by others' opinions or demands, but by His loving face turned toward me. I set healthy boundaries to honor the image and facet of God's expression that I am. I declare that I communicate my boundaries clearly and respectfully, speaking the truth in love, and seeking to build bridges and foster under-standing. I acknowledge that my time is a gift from God and

I steward it wisely, ensuring I have time for rest, personal growth, and meaningful connections.

I surrender my emotions to Yahweh. I establish boundaries to protect my emotional well-being and stability, disallowing others to manipulate my feelings. I commission angels to help me in this regard. Let it be known that I am empowered to say 'no' when necessary. I will not overcommit nor take on more than I can handle or desire. I declare that my ultimate Source of strength and guidance comes from God Most High, and I hereby establish boundaries to create space for prayer, meditation and seeking His will as I co-create my destiny with Him. Let it be so.

Love, Joy and Peace

Combo:

Creator and Father who loves me, I receive your love into every facet of my being. I position myself in the streams of everlasting love that flow from your throne, and I allow the frequencies of love, joy and overwhelming peace to wash over me and through me. I release any tension, worry or striving. I surrender it all to you—my ashes for your beauty. Please forgive me for the times I've not acted loving to people, or to myself. Forgive me for bringing or allowing strife and confusion when I could have shifted the atmosphere to peace and harmony by my words and actions. Please show me if there are wounds in me that trigger hurt and resentment that block the flow of your love and joy. Help me heal them. I'm ready to let them go for your greater purpose and plan for my life and business. Show me who I am without those false structures I've built stories on. Show me myself as I truly am—fully loved, filled with joy, and going through my day in complete peace.

I declare that I shift atmospheres wherever I go, bringing Heaven's hope and joy to people and places. I release love and peace to those around me today and everyday, in person and online, through all my communication channels, and wherever my content is seen and heard. I decree and declare they will leave any interaction with me more peaceful, joyful, hope-filled and inspired. In the Name who is Love itself, amen.

Bonus Prayers and Declarations

When your Business is Stuck or Under Attack

Quick review from the *Tips on Engaging Your Destiny Scroll* section earlier:

What to do if there's just nothingness when you are listening or watching for answers. There may be bondages that keep you from seeing. There may be deeper roots that need to be pulled out, but here's the quick fix to try first. Name whatever it is: Blankness, Blackness, Nothingness, etc. Say, "Blackness, what right do you have to be here?" Listen/feel for an answer. You may hear a word such as "unforgiveness" or "doubt" or "anger", or you may feel resentment or some other negative emotion. Name the emotion or say the word you heard, and ask Jesus to forgive you for coming into agreement with it. Say out loud that you break agreement with it. Give it to Jesus. Receive your forgiveness. Declare yourself forgiven and free. And look again. Usually this opens your ability to connect, but it could also take a few rounds if there are layered obstacles blocking you. If you need help, I'm available. *Book a Liebust session with me here: SpiritCenteredBusiness.com/healing*

This is my "go-to" when there seems to be something amiss in my business, and that of my clients. Typically your external world is a reflection of your inner world. Fear, doubt, unworthiness, fear of rejection, shame and guilt are business show stoppers. Look inside first. If your inner world seems to be okay, then check your discipline. Are you doing the things you know to do? Are you creating with intention, or are you creating chaos by NOT intentionally creating? (We're ALWAYS creating by our words and actions and dominant emotional state.)

Sometimes I like to take communion before I press in to an encounter with the Lord. If you anticipate a full on, deal-with-my-schtuff session, go ahead and pray the *Opening/ Covering* prayer from chapter 4, and use the protocols to "step into" heaven to get 'er done.

Deal with Inner World Issues

Source of all, you see what's going on in my business right now. Please show me if there's anything in me that I need to let you deal with. (Wait...listen...watch with your spiritual eyes and be prepared to take notes.)

When something negative comes to mind:

Jesus, please forgive me for coming into agreement with _____. I nail them to your cross where your blood can wash them completely away. I break that agreement now and come out of alignment with all the associated lies. I forgive anyone involved, and I ask you to forgive them too. I receive my forgiveness and declare myself and my business completely free in your mighty Name.

Do this until nothing more comes up...or get a whole list and break agreement all at the same time.

Combo:

Father God, I know you see the struggles in my business, and the challenges we face. I believe I have done the inner work you highlighted to me to the best of my ability. If there is anything else I need to deal with, I trust you will bring it to my attention. Right now I am standing on the promises that you showed me when I saw the destiny scroll for my business. If I missed you, please give me confirmation. In the meantime I will continue stewarding this mandate, and I need your help. I know that the battle we face is not against flesh and blood, but against spiritual forces of darkness. I declare your divine protection and intervention over my business and all its interests. I commission warring angels to guard and defend every aspect of it from any spiritual attack. Lord, rebuke any negative and harmful influences that seek to hinder the success and growth of this venture. I break any curses spoken over this business. Let them fall lifeless to the ground. I make no agreement with them.

I declare the power of the blood of Jesus Christ over my business, sealing it from all evil intentions and malevolent forces. May your light shine brightly in every corner, dispelling any darkness that tries to infiltrate. Grant me discernment and wisdom to recognize and resist any deceptive schemes or strategies of the enemy. I declare that my team and I have the perseverance to overcome every obstacle and to fulfill the purpose you have for this business. I surrender the burdens of this situation into your hands, knowing that you are my CEO seated on your throne, and nothing is too difficult for you. Your power is greater than any spiritual attack we may face. Lord, please strengthen my resolve and that of my team, so we may continue to work diligently and faithfully to bring you glory and honor. Let it be so.

Prayer to Accept Jesus as Your Savior and Lord

When you're ready to give your heart to the Lord and start the journey of becoming a maturing son, king and priest, this prayer is all you need to begin.

Prayer:

God, I admit that I'm not perfect. I mess up, I do things that don't please you, and I need help. I'm ready to change and do life differently. I want to live in your plans and purposes for my life. Jesus, I believe you are the true Son of God, that you came to earth as a human, lived a sinless life, were crucified, died and were buried. I believe you triumphed over death and came back to life victorious to save me from hell. I choose you to be my Savior and Lord, and to live in me from today on. Fill me with your love and light, and help me to become a loving person like you. Restore me to a right relationship with God. Thank you, Jesus. In your Name I pray. Amen.

Next you'll want to connect with people who have solid biblical teaching without the burden and bondage of religion. Pray and ask Jesus, or Father, or Holy Spirit—whomever you resonate with—where you can find your tribe. Look for people who are safe, because none of us are perfect.

Daily Cleansing and Blessing Everything You Put in or on Your Body

I say this in the morning with my 1st cup of coffee, and just trust that it covers my supplements, toothpaste, lotion and everything else I come into contact with throughout the day. I envision it even wiping out harmful endocrine disruptors or pesticides, herbicides and gunk in the air I breathe, as well as laundry detergents, and so on. You can apply it to anything and everything—it only takes 90 seconds.

Combo:

Father, thank you for your provision. I honor you as the Source of every good thing in my life. Please bless everything I take into, or put onto my body today. I declare it blessed. I release the frequency of heaven over it and call it back into its original God-given design, destroying any synthetics, technology and/or hybridization. I establish a filtration system that breaks any curses and catches any nefarious substance tethered to it in the physical or spiritual realms that would cause harm to my being. I declare they fall lifeless to the ground now, and be completely removed.

I declare that anything I inhale, intake, or absorb is beneficial to life and wellbeing. Let it be fuel for me, and add vitality, energy and vigor to my body, soul and spirit. Let it heal my body, repairing every cell: bones, muscles, organs, nerves, tissues and systems. I declare that everything I put into or onto my body today will stimulate health and youthfulness. Let it restore and reset my DNA, RNA and genome back to their original design. I declare that it purges out any harmful, unwanted substance and anything not part of my Godly design. Let these be flushed out of every system and cell now, in the mighty name of Jesus. So it shall be.

Drink a full glass of water...and you might want to stay near a bathroom! ☺

Also, sometimes as we detox, the body releases stuff that can be unpleasant. Don't worry, it's just the cleansing process, and it's all good. Keep drinking water and standing on the promise that your words are powerful. Once this prayer becomes a habit for you, it will prevent more than clean up, which is a very good thing.

SECTION THREE
Conclusion and What's Next

CHAPTER 9

WRAPPING UP, AND NEXT STEPS

Daily Action Guide to Manifest God's Divine Plan

Most of us don't have time to go through every declaration every day. So here is a general, bare minimum prayer/declaration you can say every day. This is my roll out of bed prayer.

Morning Prayer and Declaration Combo:

Father God, creator of the universe, thank you for this day. I love you, and I welcome you into my life and work. I trust that you have already provided for my every need today. Please remove and cancel anything that happened during my sleep that is not part of my destiny. I declare this day blessed, productive, and joy-filled. I bless my body, I bless my soul, and I bless my spirit. I bless everything I consume today. I put on my personal armor*, and I reinforce protection and blessings over everything under my stewardship. I commission my angels to read my scroll for today and order my steps. Please put things in front of me that I need to see, and keep distractions far from me. Don't let me miss anything you're doing on my behalf. I expect miracles today! Let it be so, in Jesus' name. Amen.

Then you may ask which area of your personal life or business needs additional prayer or declarations, and just focus on those. Remember that these written prayers and declarations are just a jumping off point. Let Heaven show you how to expand or laser focus them.

* From Ephesians 6

The Armor of God
(from The Passion Translation)

> Now my beloved ones, I have saved these most important truths for last: Be supernaturally infused with strength through your life-union with the Lord Jesus. Stand victorious with the force of his explosive power flowing in and through you. Put on God's complete set of armor provided for us, so that you will be protected as you fight against the evil strategies of the accuser! Your hand-to-hand combat is not with human beings, but with the highest principalities and authorities operating in rebellion under the heavenly realms. For they are a powerful class of demon-gods and evil spirits that hold this dark world in bondage. Because of this, you must wear all the armor that God provides so you're

protected as you confront the slanderer,
*for **you are destined for all things and will rise***
***victorious.** Put on truth as a belt to strengthen*
you to stand in triumph. Put on holiness as the
protective armor that covers your heart.
Stand on your feet alert, then you'll always be
ready to share the blessings of peace. In every
battle, take faith as your wrap-around shield, for
it is able to extinguish the blazing arrows coming
at you from the evil one! Embrace the power of
salvation's full deliverance, like a helmet to
protect your thoughts from lies. And take the
mighty razor-sharp Spirit-sword of the spoken
word of God. Pray passionately in the Spirit, as
you constantly intercede with every form of
prayer at all times. Pray the blessings of God
upon all his believers.

—Ephesians 6:10-18 (TPT)

Also: Isaiah 59:17 (AMP)

For He [the LORD] put on righteousness like a coat of armor, And salvation like a helmet on His head; He put on garments of vengeance for clothing And covered Himself with zeal [and great love for His people] as a cloak.

I include these scriptures so you can envision each piece of the armor you are putting on as you pray the daily prayer above. You may even want to make the physical gestures of putting each piece on so they become even more real to you.

Like any new habit we're just beginning, the more support and guardrails around you, the better. I can't tell you how many times I've started a thing, and simply forgot that I had started it because my default routines, habits and patterns just took over when I wasn't paying attention.

Tools you may choose to use:

- Paper and pen tracking spreadsheet
- Good old-fashioned day planner
- Apps you can input the habit you want to do every day and get reminders
- Alarms or timers
- Sticky notes
- Dry erase calendars

Whatever guardrails you put in place, though, will only work IF YOU USE THEM!

TIP: (and cautionary note) Don't try to change several habits at once. Be patient with yourself and the process. Choose one or two things to add, and one or two things to subtract. Stick with those for at least 21 days—63 days to really change your life, according to premier neuroscientist Caroline Leaf. Then move on to a couple more adds and subs and do it again.

You can do this!!

CONSISTENCY IS KEY!

...and did I mention...

CONSISTENCY IS KEY!

Travel Your Business Destiny Journey in Community

Growing and stretching and moving the needle forward in your business and life is much more fun, and often easier together. Share the vision with two or three close peers who are also running the race toward their destiny. (NOT with the negative Nellys who nay-say and drain your energy!) You can dream with each other and hold each other accountable to those dreams and milestone goals. You can also create a small mastermind group, as Napoleon Hill described in his flagship book, *Think and Grow Rich*. When two or more are gathered in Yahweh's name, He promises to be in their midst.

Using the protocols from Section One, step into the heavenly business center and use a conference room in your office. (Part of your Deed of Commerce and Trade.) Invite Jesus and other assistants in to see what is on your CEO's heart, figure out solutions to problems, and receive strategy from Heaven. This is a powerful practice! As I've shared testimonies throughout this book, I'm sure you've picked up that this is how I run my business and help my clients run theirs as well.

Invitation to Join Spirit-Centered Business™

Business Ekklesia Group

It's always nice to be part of a like-minded tribe for support and encouragement as we sojourn through life. We currently have a Business Ekklesia that meets twice a month to legislate over business and engage with Jesus, our business scrolls and the heavenly beings assigned to us. I try not to teach or coach, but just facilitate stepping into the business complex together to see what Heaven has for us. As we grow we will offer more of these ekklesia groups so that the number of participants remains small and intimate. We've become family, and we intercede for each other as well. See SpiritCenteredBusiness.com/activation for details.

SCB Programs and Memberships

In addition to our FREE Facebook tribe, we have various programs, bootcamps, challenges and events throughout the year in Spirit-Centered Business™. One of the new initiatives we're working on is a health and longevity membership with in-person events for healing and wellness. Make sure you're on our mailing list. Just sign up for any of the FREE products on the website, and you'll automatically get all the news and tips. Also check the website to see what's going on now, and what's coming up. Join us on Facebook! http://facebook.com/groups/scbtribe

Share Your Testimony

Thank you for choosing *Discover Your Business Destiny* to learn how to receive and engage your scroll and partner with Heaven. Would you please help other people discover this book by sharing your testimony of how doing these activations helped or transformed your business so they, too, can bring heaven to earth? I would appreciate that so much! Go to SpiritCenteredBusiness.com/business-destinybook to leave your comments. You may also post your testimony wherever you find us on social media. Thank you!

CHAPTER 10

COOL STUFF IN THE BACK OF THE BOOK

Resources/Recommended Reading

(Note: Some of these resources are non-Christian or Jesus-plus. Use discernment.)

- *Breaking the Habit of Being Yourself* by Joe Dispenza
- *Caught Up in the Spirit* by Christopher Paul Carter
- *Hearing God* by Dallas Willard
- *How to Own Your Own Mind* by Napoleon Hill
- *Miracles are Normal: Co-Creating Through Oneness with God* by Virginia Killingsworth
- *Napoleon Hill's Golden Rules* by Napoleon Hill
- *Planning to Profit: Architecting Your Unique Story into a Business You Love* by Bralynn Newby
- *Switch on Your Brain* by Dr. Caroline Leaf
- *The Complete Works of Florence Scovel Shinn* by Florence Scovel Shinn
- *The Divine Matrix* by Gregg Braden

- *The Fourth Dimension* by Dr. David Yonggi Cho
- *The Intention Experiment* by Lynne McTaggart
- *The Power of Your Subconscious Mind* by Joseph Murphy
- *The Science of Miracles: Re-Membering the Frequency of Love* by Dr. Sharnael Wolverton Sehon
- *Understanding the Power of Your Mind* by Joe Dispenza
- *Unlocking Destinies from the Courts of Heaven* by Robert Henderson

Kingdom Concepts

As I promote this book and in the weeks and months to follow its release, I would like to build a library of short teachings on concepts I have alluded to in the prayers and declarations above. Most of us were not taught these biblical principles in church. I know I wasn't. Also, since we've transitioned into the Kingdom Age, we're in a new age of dispensation of revelation beyond what the Church Age received. I don't have all the answers, and maybe I only have a partial understanding of a principle, but I'm happy to share what I have and keep on growing and learning right along with you. We will put the link to these teachings on the website. Check SpiritCenteredBusiness.com/business-destinybook for new releases.

Also Recommended for Study

For a solid Biblical foundation and excellent teaching on some of the ways we can operate in the spirit realm, visit

Virgina Killingsworth's playlist on YouTube, called *Restoring the Ancient Pathways*.

https://www.youtube.com/playlist?list=PLzS9x76-mP-Cpj1qHTrCo0Krrg6KkjuIW

DECLARATION OF TRADE

Online Course Bundle

This Do-It-Yourself course includes:

The Destiny Scroll Guided Activation

to receive and read/engage your scroll and

The Declaration of Trade Online Course

to establish your business in heaven for protection, resources and strategy

PLUS:

You have the option of grabbing an Activation session with Bralynn at a discount to help you get your documentation approved in Heaven.

Visit

SpiritCenteredBusiness.com/declaration

SPIRITUAL BUSINESS COACHING

Partner with Heaven to remove barriers to success and establish and operate a Kingdom business on earth. We work with Kingdom business owners who want the fullness of what Father God has for them.

Whether you need Heaven's strategy to build or scale your company, boost productivity, or implement systems—or Holy Spirit's help through your toughest challenges, our coaching provides the spiritual and practical support you need for freedom, success and forward momentum on your destiny.

- Access the heavenly realm for resources, strategy, and assistance, then pull it down to build it on earth.
- Clean up ancestral and personal limitations to success, clearing and shifting our mindset and energy to move forward unhindered in confidence.
- Engage the destiny scroll of your business and establish your Declaration of Trade (covenant partnership agreement with Heaven) and other founding documents to ensure full protection, rights and access to heaven.
- Deploy and commission the angels assigned to your business.
- Step into your role as King and Priest.

MENU OF SERVICES

- **Personal Liebusting**
  Inner and physical healing, and bloodline cleansing
- **Business Liebusting**
  Cleanse foundation, break barriers, unlock revelation (also territory, events, and more)
- **Activation Coaching**
  Partner with Heaven in any area of life
- **Building with Heaven Coaching**
  For coaches, speakers and influencers to bottle their brilliance and fulfill their destiny through their business. (See also BralynnNewby.com)
- **Fusion Coaching**
  Combines healing, Courts of Heaven, and business coaching with a trained seer
- **Group Equipping and Coaching**
  Various programs and memberships to learn and grow in community
- **Build It Business Services**
  Virtual assistants: website, tech integration, video production, social media posting, and more.

SpiritCenteredBusiness.com/Coaching

AWAKENING & EQUIPPING

We offer various group programs and memberships where you can encounter Jesus, discover your inheritance as a son, and dive into God's deeper mysteries in a safe, yet iron sharpening environment.

Some Topics We Explore and Implement
- Sanctified Imagination
- Reality of Father's Kingdom
- Activating your Human Spirit
- Soul Parts and Integration
- Spirit, Soul and Body Healing and Longevity
- Expanding your Inner Structures
- Abundance Mindset
- Personal and Business Mountains
- Trading Floors and Trade Routes
- Identity: Sonship, Kingship and Priesthood
- Business Complex of Heaven
- Timeline Recalibration
- Pulling Heaven to Earth
- Courts, Legal Issues and Legislating from Heaven
- Thrones and Dual Citizenship
- Working with Angels and People in White
- Lingering Human Spirits
- ...and more as Holy Spirit reveals!

Call to Me and I will answer you, and tell you
[and even show you] great and mighty things,
[things which have been confined and hidden],
which you do not know and understand and cannot distinguish.

—Jer 33:3 (AMP)

It is the glory of God to conceal a matter,
But the glory of kings is to search out a matter.

—Prov 25:2

Join Us and Transform Your Life!
SpiritCenteredBusiness.com

SPIRIT-CENTERED BUSINESS™ PODCAST

Partnering with Heaven
for Supernatural Results on Earth.

The Kingdom Age of doing business by being Spirit-Centered is coming together in collaboration, working with Yahweh's spiritual principles, knowing our identity and our destiny. We showcase entrepreneurs, leaders and business professionals who blend their faith and spirituality with their work to walk out their destiny through their business.

SpiritCenteredBusiness.com/Podcast

Find Us, Like, Subscribe, Follow and Share
on YouTube, Facebook, Rumble, Spotify

and other popular platforms.

www.ingramcontent.com/pod-product-compliance
Lightning Source LLC
Chambersburg PA
CBHW070039100426
42740CB00013B/2732